Praise for *How We Ma*

"Roger Cross knows kids. I worked with him in Youth for Christ for many years. This book draws on his experience as a youth worker and father and is filled with practical advice to help anyone in close proximity with kids. I highly recommend this book."

KEN DAVIS, host of the radio show *Lighten Up!*

"What an amazingly practical book. Roger Cross doesn't waste a word on a single page. This book delivers straightforward solutions to clearly diagnosed problems. Roger gets to the heart of the issue from a biblically tested point of view and delivers ideas that allow sustainable change to take place."

DANIEL S. WOLGEMUTH, President/CEO, Youth for Christ/USA, Inc.

"There's no doubt from my travels today that Roger has hit on a very important subject for parents. I come in contact with a lot of angry kids, and this book will help parents address this critical issue."

DENNY RYDBERG, President, Young Life

"Roger Cross leads the way with his own transparency, humility and experience. He offers revealing insights on common parent challenges and does it in an empathetic and nonjudgmental way. In so doing, Roger gives us the advantage of his valuable lessons from hindsight that can benefit all of us—even some of us grandparents!"

PAUL FLEISCHMANN, President, National Network of Youth Ministries

"Few parents intentionally set out to *make* their children angry. But we *can*—and we *do*. Roger Cross lifts the shade on some unintentional behaviors that we can avoid in parenting."

ELISA MORGAN, CEO, MOPS International

"Dealing with unhealthy anger is the number one issue that causes parents to come for family counseling. This book is an invaluable gift for every married and single parent. The chapter on how parents can be on the same page is by itself worth the price of the book. I know that this is a book you will read more than once and one you'll want to share with your friends."

DR. GARY J. OLIVER, Executive Director, The Center for Relationship Enrichment, and coauthor of *Raising Sons and Loving It*

HOW WE MAKE OUR KIDS ANGRY

Suggestions for Parents

Who Want to Change

Roger Cross

with Ed Stewart

IVP Books

An imprint of InterVarsity Press

Downers Grove, Illinois

InterVarsity Press
P.O. Box 1400, Downers Grove, IL 60515-1426
World Wide Web: www.ivpress.com
E-mail: email@ivpress.com

InterVarsity Press® is the book-publishing division of InterVarsity Christian Fellowship/USA®, a student movement active on campus at hundreds of universities, colleges and schools of nursing in the United States of America, and a member movement of the International Fellowship of Evangelical Students. For information about local and regional activities, write Public Relations Dept., InterVarsity Christian Fellowship/USA, 6400 Schroeder Rd., P.O. Box 7895, Madison, WI 53707-7895, or visit the IVCF website at <www.intervarsity.org>.

All Scripture quotations, unless otherwise indicated, are taken from the Holy Bible, New International Version®. NIV®. *Copyright ©1973, 1978, 1984 by International Bible Society. Used by permission of Zondervan Publishing House. All rights reserved.*

The list on page 62 is reprinted from The Seven Cries of Today's Teens *by Timothy Smith. Copyright ©2003 by Timothy Smith. Used by permission of Timothy Smith.*

Material on pages 67-68 is taken from Boundaries with Kids *by John Townsend; Henry Cloud. Copyright ©1998 by Henry Cloud and John Townsend. Used by permission of Zondervan.*

Quotes on pages 76-77 and the table on page 78 are reprinted from Parenting with Love & Logic. *©1990 by Foster Cline, M.D. and Jim Fay. Used by permission of NavPress, Colorado Springs, CO (www.navpress.com). All rights reserved. Material on pages 77-81 is also adapted from* Parenting with Love & Logic.

The excerpt on pages 111-14 from How to Parent with Your Ex *©2005 by Brette McWhorter Sember, is used by permission of its publisher, Sphinx Publishing.*

Every effort has been made to obtain permission for material quoted in the book. The author will be pleased to rectify any omissions in future editions if notified by the copyright holders.

Design: Cindy Kiple
Images: Joseph Devenney/Getty Images

ISBN 978-0-8308-3365-8

Printed in the United States of America ∞

Library of Congress Cataloging-in-Publication Data

Cross, Roger, 1943
   How we make our kids angry: suggestions for parents who want to
change / Roger Cross.
      p. cm.
   Includes bibliographical references.
   ISBN 978-0-8308-3365-8 (pbk.: alk. paper)
   1. Anger—Religious aspects—Christianity. 2. Parenting—Religious
aspects—Christianity.3. Parent and child—Religious
aspects—Christianity. 4. Parents—Religious life. I. Title.
   BV4627.A5C76 2007
   248.8'45—dc22

                                                                        2007021642

P	19	18	17	16	15	14	13	12	11	10	9	8	7	6	5	4	3	2	1
Y	23	22	21	20	19	18	17	16	15	14	13	12	11	10	09	08	07			

Contents

Acknowledgments

There have been many contributors to this effort. I'm especially grateful to the young people who participated in the surveys I conducted. I'm equally appreciative of the parents who willingly shared their experiences.

Along the way I have sought input from professional counselors. I wanted to make sure I was giving correct information, and these people provided illustrations and stories that found their way into these pages. Each of them is a great friend and talented in his or her field of therapy. My deep thanks to Anna Jones, Jack Nicholson, Gary Oliver and Wes Roberts.

This book could not have been written without the training and experiences I enjoyed during my career in Youth for Christ. Thanks to all my dear friends who labor tirelessly in this movement to help young people around the world.

Thanks to my dear family. I have a rich heritage from both my parents and my wife's father and mother. My children are *the best*. I love and admire all of you deeply. You have been my greatest teachers.

My wife, Jan, is responsible for so much good in the raising of our children. I was often good at exemplifying the anger generators presented in this book. My wife, on the other hand, was intuitively good at minimizing the anger. She is a "Proverbs 31 woman." I love you, Honey.

Finally, Ed Stewart is a Christian writer and longtime friend who also happens to be our older daughter's father-in-law. Ed brought his writing skills to the table to help make the manuscript more readable. Thanks, Ed!

"Sometimes You Make Me So Mad!"

I remember one of the first times our youngest daughter, Amber, vented her anger at me for something I did. In reality, it was something I *didn't* do that made her mad. She had asked me to help her with a paper she was writing for a middle school class. The paper required a lot of research, and Amber didn't know how to go about doing the research.

"There's nothing to it," I assured her flippantly. Then, instead of showing her what she needed to do, I simply told her to get started, explaining that she would figure out how to do the research as she went along.

She let out an exasperated sigh. "But, Dad, I don't know how to—"

"Amber, just get started," I insisted with authority, "and you'll figure it out." Then I left the room.

What I wouldn't admit to myself was that my advice didn't make any sense. It was like putting Amber in the cockpit of an airplane and saying, "Just push the throttle wide open, and by the time you reach the end of the runway you'll figure out how to get airborne." Truth be told, I just didn't want to be bothered with Amber's project. I was being lazy and selfish with my time and help, so I blew her off and hoped she could somehow finish the project without needing me to coach her.

Later I stuck my head in Amber's room and asked, "How are you doing?"

I could see the frustration and irritation in her eyes. Then she opened fire. She snapped off an angry response to my question and it went downhill from there—heated words and bitter tears. Amber had made a valiant attempt to get started. But since I hadn't given her the tools she needed, she was stuck and frustrated and angry. I'm embarrassed to say that this wasn't the only time my selfishness sparked an angry episode with Amber or my other two children.

The details may be different, but I'll bet you have a story or two like mine from your own experience with angry kids. Even when we parent with all the compassion, fairness and patience we can muster, we still do things that prompt our kids to snarl, slam doors or retreat into angry silence. And what about the many incidents like my clash with Amber when we're not very compassionate, fair or patient? Talk about parent-child fireworks!

The phenomenon of angry children and teens and how they vent their hurt and anger in their families and in society seems to be getting more serious. Angry kids have always talked back to their parents and pulled some vengeful and destructive stunts. But these days it's all too common to hear about gun-toting kids blowing away gang rivals, teachers, classmates and even family members.

I'm not addressing in this book the problem of violent anger in kids, as serious as it may be, because that's not where most of us live. However, as a youth worker and a parent, I'm deeply concerned about the everyday anger we generate unnecessarily in our children and youth and how it negatively affects them. That's why I wrote this book. I want to help parents learn to recognize how we anger our kids unnecessarily so we can stop doing it.

TWO SIDES OF A CHILD'S ANGER

There are two verses in the Bible that are directed at parents and that have always intrigued me. The apostle Paul wrote to the Christian church at Ephesus, "Fathers, do not exasperate your children; instead, bring them up in the training and instruction of the Lord" (Ephesians 6:4). He wrote a similar admonition to the believers at Colossae: "Fathers, do not embitter [provoke to anger] your children, or they will become discouraged" (Colossians 3:21).

I've wondered why God, speaking through Paul's writing, thought it important to bring up—not once, but twice—the subject of provoking anger in our kids, especially considering that there are only a handful of verses in the Bible that directly address parents and parenting. There must be a deep truth here. I believe there are two primary reasons for this dramatic emphasis.

First, we parents are skilled at making our kids mad, and dads seem to be particularly adept at it. And while there are times when our anger-producing actions are justifiable (such as when we discipline them lovingly and appropriately and they get ticked off anyway), God knows that we are prone to step over the line and anger them without just cause.

Second, provoking our kids to anger has the potential for long-lasting, negative effects in them. The Colossians verse mentions one such effect: losing heart. Kids who lose heart get discouraged with themselves, and it adversely affects their motivation. God wants us to know that uncalled-for anger in our kids can be harmful to them, so he says, "Don't do it."

"But you don't know my kid," you may argue. "If I stopped doing everything that makes him mad, he'd end up with no rules, doing anything he wants." I hear you, and you have a valid point.
Even our good and reasonable rules may cause our kids to stomp
off as if we were heartless tyrants. I'm not saying that we should
avoid doing anything that ticks off our kids, because that's not
what the Bible is saying.

The key for the two New Testament statements about anger is
found in the verses above them. Ephesians 6:1 reads, "Children,
obey your parents in the Lord, for this is right." Colossians 3:20 says,
"Children, obey your parents in everything, for this pleases the
Lord." Instructing kids to obey implies that parents are to set behavior standards that are to be obeyed. If your reasonable rules and standards provoke your kids to anger, their anger is not your fault. In the
context of your continuing love and care, they will eventually get
over it and maybe even learn to appreciate your guidance.

But sometimes the child's anger is our fault, and it's unnecessary
and harmful. That's the kind of behavior God was talking about
when he said, "Do not provoke your children to anger." I want to
help you identify ways parents provoke their kids to unnecessary
anger, and I want to show you how to avoid these hurtful behaviors.

I speak from my experience as the father of three grown children
and from thirty-eight years of ministry to tens of thousands of kids
through Youth for Christ. Also, in preparation for this book I personally interviewed over one hundred middle school, high school
and college students—and some of their parents—in different
parts of the country. The persons in this sampling represented a
wide variety of backgrounds, religious traditions, economic levels
and family situations. Their insights and questions were instru-
mental in helping me formulate the content of this book.

WHAT DO WE KNOW ABOUT ANGER?

Before we talk about the ways we provoke unnecessary anger in our kids, let's review some basic information about anger as it applies to our kids and to us.

Anger is an emotion. Like all emotions, anger is amoral—neither right nor wrong. It's OK for you to feel angry, and it's OK for your kids to feel angry. What we want to learn is how *not* to spark these angry feelings in our kids unnecessarily.

Anger is the effect of a cause. Just like us, our kids don't get angry without reason. The causes generally fall into three categories: pain (physical or emotional), frustration and fear. For example, wiping out on a skateboard can trigger an angry outburst from a kid, as can being yelled at or ignored by a parent. One of the keys to dealing with our kids' anger is to discover and address the underlying pain, frustration and/or fear—even if we are part of that cause.

Anger must be expressed appropriately. The apostle Paul wrote, "In your anger, do not sin" (Ephesians 4:26). In other words, it's OK to be angry and to express your anger; just don't do it in the wrong way. In fact, it's very important to vent our angry feelings constructively. Countless medical studies reveal a close relationship between buried emotions and physical illness.

The key to expressing anger is to do it appropriately. The kid who fails an algebra exam may respond inappropriately by racing his car up to eighty miles per hour on the highway or punching his little brother or drop kicking the dog over the fence. Or he could let off steam positively by shooting hoops for half an hour. Kids often cannot avoid getting angry, but they can decide to vent it constructively—and so can we.

Anger is often expressed toward the wrong object. You have an argument with your child, so she slams her door and trashes her bedroom. The causes of her anger aren't the door or the bedroom, but they become substitutes for dealing with her anger in a positive way. When you see your child venting her anger at inanimate objects (or the poor dog), start probing for the real cause—which may even be something you have done or said.

Anger can only be controlled by the one who is angry. When you feel angry, you are the one responsible to express it appropriately. The same is true for your kids; their anger and the resulting actions are their responsibility. One helpful way to accept personal responsibility for anger is to seek help from the outside, such as from a pastor, counselor or trusted friend. This is true for our kids as well as for us. Finding help shows a willingness to acknowledge our primary role in the matter. In controlling long-held or recurring patterns of anger, however, outside professional help should be viewed as more of a necessity than an option.

Anger can be good. Anger is energy, and energy used in the right way can accomplish a lot of good. Channeled anger can protect you from physical danger or confront injustice. I would suggest that many of the great, noble causes of history were the result of anger channeled appropriately. Martin Luther King Jr. got mad at racism and launched the Civil Rights Movement. Americans are incensed at terrorism, so we have changed our lifestyles significantly to protect against further attacks.

I would rather see my children angry than passive. Passivity scares me. It means that my child is avoiding me and the situation. Anger gives me hope. Even if it is expressed incorrectly, at least it shows that there is life and passion. I can work with that.

ANGER GENERATED, ANGER MINIMIZED

Over my years as a parent and minister to youth and their parents, I have identified what I call *anger generators*. These are the attitudes, actions and responses in parents that often provoke unnecessary anger in their kids. Each of the ten chapters ahead focuses on one of these anger generators. Real stories drawn from my own parenting and ministry and from the experiences of others will give you a clear picture of what each anger generator looks like.

For each anger generator I will share with you an *anger minimizer.* These are proven principles to help you stop provoking unnecessary anger in your kids and start building a stronger, more trusting, more loving relationship with them.

In order to help you apply these principles in a practical way, each chapter concludes with a few questions to engage you in the process. The questions will make you think about what you really believe, internalize each anger minimizer and take a positive step toward applying each principle in your parenting.

My prayer is that your journey through these pages will awaken you to new possibilities for relating to your kids and changing your family life in a positive and enriching way.

1   Why Can't I Be Me?

Not long ago I heard about an angry high school senior who I'll call Brandon. His father is a pastor with high visibility in his denomination. In addition to his church ministry, Dad proudly serves on the board of the denomination's college. People who know them both say, "Brandon is just like his dad, and he will make a fine pastor some day." Dad wholeheartedly agrees. In fact, he expects Brandon to attend the denomination's college and follow in his career path.

Here's the problem: Dad has never asked Brandon what he wants to do with his life. Brandon loves his dad and respects his ministry, but he doesn't want to be a pastor. He is being pushed into something that's not for him, so he is starting to push back. He stunned his dad by submitting an application to a different Christian school from the one his dad is pushing. His dad is so upset over Brandon's "rebellion" that he is purposely dragging his feet with the financial aid forms requested by the school. Dad is also bad-mouthing Brandon's choice to others.

Brandon is seething about being pressured to be something he's not. He says, "I'm only applying to a Christian school to please my dad. I really want to go to a state school."

ANGER GENERATOR 1:
PRESSURING YOUR KIDS TO BE SOMETHING THEY'RE NOT

Sadly, I have seen Brandon's story played out in countless numbers of homes. Many parents try to push, cajole, nag or "guilt" their kids into a particular life direction or career path without considering their wishes or dreams. And it makes our kids angry.

Why do we push our kids to be something they are not? There are a number of motives, many of them unhealthy:

- A frustrated father pushes his child to become the next Tiger Woods because the father never succeeded as an athlete himself.

- A mom pushes her kids into high-paying careers because she is afraid her husband will not be able to provide for the family financially.

- A dad pushes his kids into prestigious careers because it will boost his self-image to say he is the father of a corporate vice president.

- A woman insists that her son study law or medicine because having a professional in the family will give her status in her social circle.

Sometimes this anger generator arises from good intentions:

- A mother funnels her son into an occupation such as social work or health care because she wants him to experience the fulfillment of serving others.

- Parents who recognize music or drama talent in their child push her into a career in the performing arts because "that's what you're made for."

- A couple desiring a happy marriage for their daughter takes it upon themselves to choose Mr. Right for her.

- A child is forced in a certain life direction because a parent is convinced it is God's will for his child.

Whatever the motive, if kids are forced to be something they are not, it will likely generate deep-seated anger, even though that anger may not come to the surface until later in life.

Parents can also generate unnecessary anger by being pushy or demanding in areas much less important than life direction and career choice. I'm talking about how we tend to micromanage our kids' preferences and behavior when it comes to their clothing, hairstyles, music, school activities, friends and so on. To be sure, we need to be actively involved and at times heavy-handed with our kids in areas that relate to safety, health, cleanliness, clear moral issues and obeying the law. But sometimes we blur the line between right and wrong and personal preference, and it drives our kids up the wall.

Why do we sometimes pressure our kids concerning their tastes and preferences, making them angry? I can think of several reasons: We sincerely want to guide them in the right direction but sometimes get a little overzealous about it. We are afraid they will get caught up in the world's value system, so we go overboard about some issues. We have a strong desire to transfer our Christian values and worldview to our kids, but at times we stretch biblical teaching to include personal tastes and preferences.

Sometimes we come down on our kids' appearance and behavior simply because it embarrasses us in front of our friends. For some parents, it's a control issue. They feel that they must lay down the law to maintain their kids' obedience and respect, which can lead to being heavy-handed in areas where more freedom might be OK.

ANGER MINIMIZER 1:
ENCOURAGING YOUR KIDS TO BECOME WHO THEY ARE

I think we all agree that every individual—adult, teenager or young child—is a unique package of talents, gifts, interests and preferences. One of our most important jobs as parents is to help our kids discover how they are wired and do all we can to encourage them to express their uniqueness in fruitful and fulfilling ways. When parents are fountainheads of loving affirmation and encouragement instead of manipulators or dictators, it produces a sense of worth and healthy self-esteem in their kids instead of anger.

ENCOURAGING LIFE CHOICES

My wife, Jan, and I have three wonderful grown children—two biological daughters and a foster son. Our older daughter, Shawna, is a choral conductor. Our younger daughter, Amber, is an artist and graphic designer. Our son, Gary, who came to live with us at age seventeen, is in the medical field. Over the years, encouraging our kids to discover their career niches has been an ongoing adventure for Jan and me.

For example, we discovered early on that Shawna had musical talent. Even as a little girl she loved to sing and perform for others. During middle school and high school she was deeply involved in musical theater. She shined on stage; it was her thing. So she decided to pursue musical theater as a career. Since Jan and I both have a bent toward music, we looked for ways to help Shawna pursue this dream.

But when Shawna got to college, she hit some bumps on the road to becoming a Broadway star. She began to question whether she wanted to live the hectic, demanding lifestyle of a professional actress. She questioned if she possessed the exceptional talent and relentless drive needed to take her to the top in an extremely competitive field. It soon became apparent to Shawna that the Broadway stage was not for her. She was sad and disappointed to give up the dream of her youth, and we felt the same way for her.

Shawna had to make some big adjustments, and her mother and I were there to help and encourage her through the transition. It was not about trying to change Shawna's talents to fit the career of musical theater; it was about encouraging her to find the niche that best suited the talents God had given her.

During her last year of college, Shawna took a conducting course, and a brand new world opened up to her. I'll never forget visiting the university and meeting with her professor. He pulled me aside and said, "Roger, she's got it!" A few minutes later I watched her conduct the choir for the first time. I cried then, and I still choke up today as I think about that moment. The professor was right. All the passion Shawna once had for musical theater flowed out through her choral conducting. She had found her niche.

You may have high hopes and big expectations for your children's future careers. But if you push your hopes and expectations instead of occupying your primary role as an encourager, you may not only thwart God's plan for your kids but damage your relationship with them by making them angry. How can you be the encourager your kids need? Here are a couple of tips.

Help your kids discover their talents and gifts. We have a two-year-old grandson named Jackson. He is Shawna's son with her husband, Ken. It's been fun for Jan and me to watch potential talents and gifts emerge as Jack grows. And surprise, he likes music! When music plays, he listens with great interest and his demeanor changes. His favorite books and toys are the ones that play music, and he loves to dance around to the music. Now, does this mean

Jack will someday be the lead guitarist in the next version of the Rolling Stones or direct a university chorale like his mom? We don't know, but his early interests give us some things to watch for and encourage.

The first place to start looking for your children's talents and gifts is in other family members. If you or your parents have a knack for music or numbers or athletics or details or writing, it is likely your kids will also show natural talent in these areas of strength. Since Jackson's dad and I both love golf, we're hoping he shows interest in it. I've already "encouraged" this potential talent by buying him a set of junior golf clubs. But if Jack shows little or no interest in golf, the worst thing we could do is pressure him to become a professional golfer. The same is true in any area where your child has minimal interest or talent. Pushing there will only make him or her angry.

I'm a great believer in personality and gift testing at the appropriate ages. There are a number of excellent tools out there that can help you uncover your child's personality traits, God-given talents, spiritual gifts and so on. For example, you might want to take advantage of the Gallup organization's *Discover Your Strengths,* the Myers-Briggs Type Indicator, the DiSC Personality Profiles and the Predictive Index.

Help your kids find their niches. As you help your kids begin to discover their strengths, the next way to defuse their anger in this area is to encourage them into activities, opportunities and even career options that play to their talents and gifts. A part of this encouragement comes in the form of the personality and gift testing mentioned above. Most good testing will not only help identify and confirm talents but suggest how these talents can be used. However, much of this process happens through experimentation.

For example, if a young child shows an interest in sports, find a place to try out that interest, such as a kids' soccer league or tennis lessons. If it's art, make sure he has plenty of drawing paper, crayons, modeling clay, colored markers and so on, and look for children's art classes in your community. If your kids like music, look for ways to start them in music training at an early age.

Early childhood music training is something my wife, Jan, has been doing for more than thirty years. We own a school called Children's Music Academy in Denver, Colorado, with branches in other cities around the country. Typically, a child enters CMA at age four and graduates at age seven. Group classes are held once a week for an hour and require parent participation and interaction. There is a two-month break during the summer. It's a wonderful way for kids and their parents to experiment with their musical abilities.

One family has been in our program for seven years. As their children have grown, the parents have enrolled the children in CMA. But get this: They live two hours away from the music studio! Thirty-six weeks a year for the past seven years these parents have made the four-hour round trip to Denver for a one-hour music class. They don't do it because their kids are extraordinarily gifted or to push them to become concert musicians. They do it because they want to give their kids the opportunity to experiment with and maximize any musical talents they have.

Can you imagine the sacrifice these and other CMA parents have made to encourage their kids in music? You will face similar sacrifices in your commitment to encourage your kids to find their niches, especially when they are very young. In the early stages you need to be more directive and participative about getting them involved in activities. As your children grow older, you may become less directive and more supportive as they discover their own opportunities for experimentation. There are limits to this, of course, because unbridled experimentation can be expensive as well as draining physically and emotionally.

Here is a guideline for working within your limitations: Make sure each new interest a child wants to explore really fits with his or her emerging talents and gifts. For example, a kid may beg you to send her to basketball camp, but if this is her first glimmer of interest in basketball, you might suggest that she plays on the team for a year to see if she really likes it before making such a big commitment to basketball.

Assure your kids that your goal is to help them discover how they are wired and to support their experimentation in these areas as much as you are able. As your kids begin to find their favorite activities and best skills, you need to work with them to decide how much time, money and energy you can devote to supporting their efforts. And as they grow older, it is not unreasonable to ask them to share in some of the costs of what they want to do.

The high school years are also a good time to explore career fairs with your student and to scout out colleges that are best suited to take his or her gifts and skills to the next level. Look for internships that may be available in your child's field of strong interest. And take the initiative to locate people in that field who can share from their experience the plusses and minuses of that career.

ENCOURAGING UNIQUENESS

In the midst of discovering their interests and gifts, children at all ages are also discovering their own unique personalities and preferences. These discoveries may be a challenge for you. For example, you may regard rap music as noise, while your middle school son enjoys it as great music—the louder the better. How will you handle that? And how will you respond if your child wants to paint his bedroom fluorescent orange or pierce his nose or bleach half her hair or campaign for the political party you don't support or whatever? You get the picture.

Encouraging your kids to be the unique persons God created them to be may mean they turn out different than you expect—perhaps a lot different. In areas where their preferences may be harmful to themselves or others, of course you must step in to protect them. But in areas that are not life-threatening, illegal or immoral, pushing them to conform to your preferences may ignite a storm of unnecessary anger.

We learned this lesson the hard way at Amber's expense. As our second child, Amber had the deck stacked against her in some ways. She and her older sister, Shawna, are wired differently. Even though Jan and I were aware that comparing Amber to her older sister was unhealthy, we fell into that trap at times.

For example, we raised our kids in church, and Shawna embraced the Christian faith easily and naturally at a young age. Not Amber. She didn't accept the Christian message at face value like Shawna did or take the same path to faith, and I was perplexed by it. Our attempts to conform her to our image of how a Christian looks and acts only provoked anger and rebellion.

Only later did we realize that Amber is a more analytical thinker than Shawna. She had to come to faith on her own terms, once it made intellectual sense to her. It took her more time, and she experienced some hard knocks along the way. But she made the transition despite her parents' sometimes overbearing attempts at persuasion. Today Amber's faith runs deep and true.

In retrospect, Jan and I now see what we could have done to encourage Amber's uniqueness. Here are a few suggestions you may find helpful in this area.

Don't unfairly compare your children. Allow each child to express his or her unique personality and tastes without insisting that one fit into the mold of another.

Praise and encourage each child's uniqueness. If a kid likes to dress in a way that is different but acceptable, buy him the kind of clothes he likes instead of forcing your own dress code.

Praise a child's unique gifts in front of others. Jan and I eventually learned to appreciate Amber's analytical personality and to communicate our praise for her uniqueness to others.

Find others exhibiting the same traits in a positive way and encourage your kids to emulate them. If your kids are into alternative music, take your kids to a concert by a Christian band in that genre or buy them CDs they like and that are acceptable.

Helping your children discover their gifts and their niches and express their uniqueness in positive ways is difficult, time-consuming, energy-draining, emotionally taxing work. But I will tell you this: It is one of the most invigorating and rewarding experiences of life. When your kids begin to flourish in their "sweet spots," enjoying the gifts and uniqueness you encouraged them to discover, your soul will soar! You will see them helping people and being fulfilled because they are doing and being what they were designed for.

And they won't be angry at you. They'll be grateful.

CONSIDER AND RESPOND

1. In what areas are you pushing your kids to be something they're not instead of encouraging them to be who they are? Why do you think you are doing it?

2. List on paper a number of the gifts, talents and preferences you see in your children. Ask your spouse to do the same without seeing your list. Compare your lists and identify the top two or three for each child.

3. Working from this composite list, how will you seek to encourage and help each of your children explore and experiment with their strengths and preferences?

2

You Have to Earn Your Stripes, Kid

Akeelah and the Bee is a fun, feel-good movie about a middle school girl from South Central Los Angeles who overcomes great odds to reach the finals of the Scripps National Spelling Bee. Encouraged by her teacher and principal, reluctant Akeelah Anderson enters a number of spelling contests and discovers her untapped talent and drive to do well. She must overcome the ridicule of friends who think spelling bees are uncool and the opposition of her single mom, who fears that the contests will distract Akeelah from her "real" schoolwork. With the help of her coach, Akeelah rises through regional and state competitions to reach the finals in Washington, D.C.

After several rounds of stiff competition, the field narrows to two finalists: Akeelah and a sour-faced boy named Dylan who previously won second place in the same competition. Dylan's path to the finals was much different than Akeelah's. His dad is obsessed with his son winning the national bee. An underachiever all his life, Dad has hounded Dylan like a Marine drill sergeant, praising him when he succeeds and berating him for even the tiniest mistake or moment of laziness. Father-son warmth is missing from their relationship; it's all about the business of winning. As a result, Dylan is very good at spelling, but he is smoldering with anger at his dad.

I won't spoil the ending for you, but at the climax of the movie Dylan's anger prompts him to do something totally unexpected that has a dramatic impact on the championship—and on his father. This conflict between Dylan and his dad illustrates the second anger generator I want to talk about. It's the anger kids feel when their parents' affection and acceptance is based on their behavior.

ANGER GENERATOR 2:
LOVING YOUR KIDS FOR WHAT THEY DO

Kids get hurt and angry when parents raise them in a performance-based environment. In this setting, as long as a kid is meeting or exceeding parental standards, he enjoys his parents' affection and attention. But when his performance isn't up to par, parental love is replaced by criticism and distance until the kid toes the line. Sometimes the demands and expectations of parents are so high— such as perfection!—that their kids can never fully meet them. As a result, they live under a dark cloud all the time, unable to please their parents and enjoy their full acceptance and love. In the film cited above, this seems to have been Dylan's experience. Such pain and hopelessness makes kids angry.

BATTLING THE ODDS

Why do we parents sometimes tend to measure out our love based on a child's performance? For one thing, some of us grew up with parents who raised us that way, so we raise our kids as we were raised. For example, as a kid maybe you brought home a report card with five As and one C, but the As went unnoticed while you got reamed out for the *C*. So now with your kids your lectures about their failures far outweigh your praise for their successes.

On a much bigger scale, we live in a society that is obsessed with winning at all costs. Whether it is in politics, business, finance, education, entertainment or sports, winners reap the power, fame, wealth and praise while losers end up with the leftovers, sometimes despised or relegated to obscurity.

Professional sports are such a glaring example of this contrast. Several years ago, Donnie Moore was the ace relief pitcher for the California Angels in their quest for the World Series. During a critical playoff game, the Angels were one strike away from victory and a Series appearance, and their ace was on the mound. But instead of delivering a game-ending strikeout, Moore gave up a game-tying home run and the Angels went on to lose the playoffs and miss the World Series.

Overnight, Donnie Moore, who had been a crowd favorite, became a hated enemy. The press and the fans were merciless in their criticism. He became the scapegoat for the perpetually underachieving Angels. The animosity against Moore was so heated that he received death threats and couldn't go out in public. And it continued into the next season. Some people think this brutal treatment contributed to Moore's suicide three years later. Others are quick to cite that Moore also suffered from clinical depression, substance abuse and a failing marriage.

Although rarely to this extreme, we also are surrounded by and sometimes caught up in the pressure to achieve and excel in life, so we pass that pressure on to our kids. We drive them to succeed, contribute, accomplish something worthwhile and perhaps even distinguish themselves in some way. When they succeed, we reward them; when they fall short, we push them harder, sometimes withholding the acceptance and encouragement they need most to succeed. We don't mean to impose this pressure; it just seems to come naturally.

Why do we feel such pressure for our kids to succeed? Because it's a dog-eat-dog world out there. It costs two arms and a leg to send a kid to college, and the competition for scholarships is fierce. There's also the social pressure. We want our kids to excel so we can "keep up with the Joneses." After all, you never see a bumper sticker that reads, "My kid is just average at Lincoln High." So we push our children to get the best grades so they can attend the best schools and land the best jobs, giving us reason to be proud.

As parents, it's right for us to encourage and praise our children. But if we only do so when they are working hard, succeeding and achieving, what are we saying about their worth? Or if we only applaud our kids for winning and not for their effort in games they lose, what are we conveying to them? Performance-based parenting says to the kid, "I love you when you excel and succeed; the rest of the time I'm not so sure." This message hurts kids and provokes them to anger.

There are two groups of people who are particularly susceptible to inflicting performance pressure on their children. The first group is fathers. As a dad, I understand this pressure firsthand. Men in general seem to be highly driven in the area of performance. We find our worth more in what we do than in who we are, and we tend to treat our kids the same way. We applaud and accept them more for their achievements than for their intrinsic worth.

You know how tough some dads can be when watching their kids play sports. I've seen dads verbally and even physically assault their sons or daughters for striking out, missing a free throw or allowing a soccer goal. That kind of treatment says much to a kid about what Dad thinks is important.

The second group is religious people who believe that right-standing with God is earned through good works. For them, ultimate success depends on good triumphing over evil in their lives, so life is all about good performance. The Pharisees of the New Testament were often rebuked by Jesus for their practice of elevating works, service and duty ahead of love, grace and faith. Even those of us whose faith is founded on the biblical doctrine of grace struggle with this issue at times. Jesus said there is nothing we can do to earn our salvation, but we still try. When people live under a works mentality, they tend to demand the same from their kids.

I grew up in a Sunday school that awarded pins for faithful attendance, but I don't remember being praised for what I learned there. I got prizes for memorizing Bible verses but received nothing when I applied those verses to my life. Jan and I fell into the same performance trap with our kids. But as they grew, we began to realize what we were communicating and shifted our emphasis to affirming them for what they learned, what they were struggling with and what questions they had.

ANGER MINIMIZER 2:
LOVING YOUR KIDS FOR WHO THEY ARE

The way to minimize the anger that results from performance-based approval is to shower our kids with praise and acceptance for who they are as much as for what they do. It's called unconditional love, the same kind of love God demonstrates toward us. Jesus said, "Love one another. As I have loved you, so you must love one another" (John 13:34). How did Christ love us? Paul writes, "While we were still sinners, Christ died for us"

(Romans 5:8). Think about it: Jesus loved us and died for us before we had done *anything* right! And that's how we are to love others, including kids whose performance is sometimes less than what we desire.

Jesus' parable of the prodigal son in Luke 15 contains a shining example of a father's unconditional love. In the story, this dad's younger son asks for his inheritance early, and Dad agrees. The young man leaves home and blows his the whole wad on reckless living. (You don't need a lot of imagination to understand what "reckless living" might include!) Suddenly destitute and remembering how good he had it at home, the boy returns to his dad, humiliated and repentant.

What would you do if your kid pulled a stunt like that—basically took half your net worth and flushed it down the toilet, then came crawling back home? Well, the father in the parable puts us all to shame. He welcomes his lost son with open arms and throws a big celebration—and doesn't say a word about the bad things his kid did. That's what it means to love without conditions or strings.

On the one hand, we must love and accept our kids unconditionally, even when their rooms are a mess, they carry a C-minus average, they back the car though the garage door, they wander far from God, they get arrested, or whatever. On the other hand, we are responsible to teach, train, discipline and correct our kids in order to keep them safe, help them succeed in life and encourage them to give their lives to God. But whether they heed the correction and training or throw it back in our faces, we love them just the same.

How can we strike a healthy balance between these potentially conflicting values of love and discipline? Let me offer several suggestions for parents of young children and for parents of teenagers.

LOVING YOUNG CHILDREN UNCONDITIONALLY

Hug and hold your children often. Tell them that you love them for who they are, not just because they put away their toys or didn't spill their milk. Especially communicate your love in the context of disciplining them. It's OK to give them a time-out for bad behavior and then go sit with them or hold them. Your loving words and touch are incredibly powerful at all times. Jan was particularly good at this with our girls. I eventually learned that hugs and touching from me, their father, had deep impact. It's kind of like they expect their moms to be that way, but when Daddy is physically affectionate—*wow!*

Don't tell your kids that they are "bad" for what they did. Clearly separate what they did from who they are. What they do—intentionally breaking a toy, hitting a playmate, telling a lie, etc.   may be bad, but they are still worthwhile.

Don't associate your love with their behavior. Saying "Daddy won't love you if you do that" is never a good way to control your child.

Tell or read stories to them that emphasize positive character traits more than good behavior. I remember Jan having conversations in the car with our girls about people who exhibited good traits. She referred to people we all knew so our girls could identify with them. These conversations reinforced what we were trying to teach. The Veggie Tales series is a good resource for affirming positive character. Watch the videos with your kids and talk about how you see those traits in them: kindness, fairness, truthfulness, etc.

Always lovingly encourage your children to do their best. Make sure they understand that you don't encourage them in order to love them more but because doing their best reinforces their intrinsic value and uniqueness.

LOVING YOUR TEENAGERS UNCONDITIONALLY

Be sure to address the issue in chapter one. If you are in some ways pushing your kids to be something they're not or unfairly controlling their preferences and tastes, your expressions of unconditional love elsewhere will seem artificial.

Talk to your teenagers as adults. Your teenagers *are* emerging adults, so you can talk to them that way. Tell them that you desire to love them unconditionally and admit to them when you fail to do so. Invite them to talk to you when they feel that your love and acceptance is being compromised because of something they have done. Also remind them that your standards for their behavior and your discipline for failing these standards are an expression of your unconditional love for them.

Talk to them about how they feel when their friends and peers outperform them in some way. Does your child feel unnoticed or underappreciated as an average student among above average friends? Does she struggle with self-image because she didn't get a part in the play or wasn't elected to council or wasn't invited to a party? These are times when you need to pour on the love and praise them for who they are. But you may not know how they're feeling if you don't ask.

Discuss with them the pros and cons of living in a performance-based culture and how they feel about the inequities they see. Reinforce to them that, even though the culture often values performance over character, you value their character above their performance.

Look for ways to demonstrate how you value their character and personality. Here are just a few ideas:

- Send them e-mails or leave sticky notes in their rooms verbalizing specific traits you appreciate. Your note might sound something like this: "I noticed your kindness today when your little sister kept interrupting you and you asked her not to in a pleasant voice."

- After they have experienced a personal disappointment or defeat, do something special to affirm your love: dinner out, shopping, a movie, a small gift, etc.

- Express your appreciation for your teenagers' character in front of their friends.

- Write a letter or prepare a video on your child's birthday. Describe their character traits in detail and let them know how thankful you are for them as persons. (I guarantee that they will keep these letters and/or videos!)

- Call your child's cell phone (she has one, doesn't she?) and leave a message. Just say that you love one of her personality or character traits and describe how you see that trait in her.

As with younger children, keep encouraging your teenagers to do their best. While endeavoring to motivate their performance, remind them that their success doesn't make them more lovable; it's merely an expression of their character, talent and discipline.

Perhaps the most significant thing you can do to create an environment of unconditional love for your children is to live daily in the light of God's unconditional love for you. As you grow in relating to God based on his unconditional acceptance of you instead of whether you succeed or fail in your work for him, you will be freer to relate to your kids with the love and acceptance that will fill them with peace instead of hurt and anger.

CONSIDER AND RESPOND

1. Think about your childhood. To what degree did your parents

condition their love and acceptance based on your perfor-mance? How did that make you feel?

2. To what degree is your love and acceptance of your children conditional upon how well they perform? What influences have contributed most to this way of relating to them?

3. Which of the suggestions for loving kids unconditionally men-tioned in this chapter do you think will be most helpful to build-ing your ability in this area? Which one would you like to follow through on first? When will you begin?

3

Playing Favorites

Alan was a second-born child. Being number two in the family can often be tough. It certainly was for him.

Alan's older brother, Alec, was like many firstborns—outgoing, a natural leader, self-assured. He was good academically and excellent in athletics, lettering in three high school sports and earning All-America football honors. He never had a problem attracting girls. His parents, Bob and Roberta, were always receiving compliments about him. More than once they heard, "Alec might be president some day."

Alan was quieter and possessed artistic skills, especially for oil painting. He rarely received the kind of public attention and recognition that his older brother did. After college, Alan decided to become a pastor. At first he liked the challenge and was relatively successful. But then his life slowly began to fall apart. He gained excessive weight, became addicted to a prescription drug and battled depression. He finally ended up in the hospital after a breakdown.

Treatment revealed that Alan had been deeply hurt over his upbringing. He knew his parents loved him, but he never felt that he measured up to his older brother. It seemed to him that Alec always got more attention from their parents, and the deeply buried hurt and anger ate at him like a cancer.

Alan's sad story is a classic case of what can happen when parents favor one child over another. Bob and Roberta were shocked at Alan's diagnosis. They loved their children dearly and were unaware that they had given Alec more attention. Yet in unseen, subtle ways they had made a distinction between Alan and Alec, and Alan paid a dear price for it.

ANGER GENERATOR 3:
FAVORING SOME CHILDREN OVER OTHERS

It is not uncommon for parents to favor one child over another. Favoritism can be intentional or unintentional. It can be obvious or subtle. It can be the result of pure motives or come out of pure selfishness. It doesn't usually mean that we love one child more than another or wouldn't lay down our lives for one and not another. It simply means that, for some reason, we are occasionally or frequently inclined toward one above another. And when children sense this disparity, especially when they are the "Alan" in the situation, they become hurt and angry.

How does parental favoritism show itself? Here are a number of acts and actions that betray our tendencies to favor one child over another.

- You give most of your time or your best time to the child who is most demanding.

- When you introduce your children to others, your favoritism may be evident in your voice inflection and excitement as you say something like, "And this is our straight-A child!"

- You are physically more affectionate with one child than the others.

- When talking about your children with your friends you show more enthusiasm about one than the others.

- Your discipline may be more lenient with one than the others.

- Your conversations are more engaging when talking with a favored child.

- One child receives more or better gifts from you.

- You refer to the "less favored" child by the name of the "more favored" child.

- You are more patient and give greater grace to one child than the others.

- You are more critical of one child than the others.

I think parents are often unaware that they favor a child or that their actions convey favoritism. I believe all parents send this message at one time or another, usually inadvertently. We're human, and we're vulnerable to playing favorites at times. But it is important to be aware if a pattern of favoritism develops over time. Perhaps even more important is being aware if a child *feels* that he or she is being less favored, even though this can be hard to detect. Feeling disfavored by a parent can be very subjective, but it can often be traced to a parent's unwitting word or act. So it is important to watch for signs that our kids are feeling less valued than their siblings.

THE FAVORITISM TRAP

Why do parents show favoritism, even when we are categorically against it? Let me share four ways we can become caught in this trap.

Favoring kids because of their traits. In his classic, *The Birth Order Book,* Dr. Kevin Leman identifies four large categories of traits and abilities that people possess. He asserts that every person tends to fall into one category. Look through the traits and abilities in the four categories below. Which category do you think best summarizes you? Your spouse? Each of your children?

A. perfectionist, reliable, conscientious, list maker, well organized, hard driving, natural leader, critical, serious, logical, doesn't like surprises, loves computers.

B. mediator, compromising, diplomatic, avoids conflict, independent, loyal to peers, many friends, a maverick, secretive, unspoiled.

C. manipulative, charming, blames others, attention seeker, tenacious, people person, natural salesperson, precocious, engaging, affectionate, loves surprises.

D. little adult by age seven; very thorough; deliberate; high achiever; self-motivated; fearful; cautious; voracious reader; black and white thinker; uses "very," "extremely," "exactly" a lot; can't bear to fail; have very high expectations for self; more comfortable with people who are older or younger.

Clarifying that there are always exceptions, Leman states that these traits are grouped according to birth order. The characteristics listed in category A are generally those found in firstborns. Traits in category B relate more to middle children, those in C are for last-borns, and those in D relate to the only child. Did the category you chose for you match your birth order? How about the categories you chose for your spouse and children?

Now, imagine that medical science could develop to the point that couples could choose the kind of child they want based on these four lists of traits. Do you think every couple would choose the same kind of child? Of course not. In fact, potential mothers and fathers might have strong disagreements over which group of traits to select. Just think how hard it is to choose a name. Now you're selecting a collection of traits!

Parents cannot predetermine the mix of characteristics and abilities in their children, of course. But we often show favoritism to children whose abilities and traits we most like or identify with. Sometimes that means we gravitate toward the kids who are most like us. For example, if you're a firstborn CEO, you might have more in common with your firstborn natural leader than with your maverick second-born, opening the door to preferential treatment. Or you may gravitate toward the child whose traits show the greatest promise for achievement and success in life. Or you may be more lenient and loving toward a compliant child than with a strong-willed, aggressive high achiever.

If you find yourself drawn to the abilities of one child over another, you're perfectly normal. It's just not OK for you to translate your preferences into favoritism.

Favoring kids because of their temperament. Temperament is about a child's attitude and approach to life. Let's face it: Nobody likes being around a kid who is always negative and picky. Sometimes we show favoritism to a kid who is easygoing, positive, happy and helpful while subtly avoiding or ignoring the kid who seems to be a drain.

Having worked with kids most of my life, I know what it means to be drawn to those who have a positive way of handling themselves and life. It is pleasant being with kids who speak respectfully and are eager to learn. It is more fulfilling to interact with a young person who can articulate what he is feeling and what he believes. It energizes me to be around kids who see the glass half full rather than half empty.

More than one parent has sheepishly confessed to me that they like being around some kids more than others because "they are just more fun." This is real life, so accept it. But we cannot treat our kids differently just because of temperament. It only makes things worse for them and for the family.

Favoring kids because of your own needs. Some parents favor certain children in order to deal with their own issues, which is inappropriate and unhealthy for parent and child. For example, a woman may be overly affectionate with her son because some of her needs are not being met by her husband. A divorced father may take unfair advantage of his daughter to meet his need for female companionship. A woman may favor her daughters in order to build in them a sense of obligation to provide attention and care for her in old age. A dad may favor his sons because he wants someone to talk football with or because he feels insecure around his daughters.

Favoring kids because of their physical appearance. We are all guilty of making judgments about people based on their physical appearance. I find myself doing this in airports while watching people I don't know. I see a woman dressed to the hilt and assume that she is a snob. I see a teenager with purple hair and metal dangling from different parts of his body and conclude that he's probably into drugs and not an honor student at school. I hear a young mother loudly scold her child and judge that the family is dysfunctional.

It may be difficult to admit, but some parents wrongly favor a child on the basis of his or her physical appearance. We may subconsciously devote more of ourselves to the child who has the better chance of winning a beauty pageant or who dresses nicer or who doesn't get into body piercing and tattoos or who controls his weight. Often this kind of favoritism is reinforced by the compliments of others, such as, "She has such beautiful hair" or "Your little boy's dimples are to die for."

This kind of favor can also work in reverse. Parents may invest more of themselves in a disabled child than in their "normal" children. It is not uncommon for the siblings of a physically challenged child to feel slighted or neglected. Such over-attention is likely not intentional; it just happens because the needy child requires it. But the other kids can feel the pain.

ANGER MINIMIZER 3:
FAVORING ALL CHILDREN EQUALLY—AS MUCH AS POSSIBLE

Favoring your kids equally is really an unreachable goal. You can try to give Christmas presents to each child that cost exactly the same, make sure you give the same amount of time to each child down to the minute and compliment them equally. But that kind of paranoia can drive you up the wall. Besides, for all your trying you will surely fail in some other area where equal favoritism is needed or expected. Let me suggest three general steps to minimizing favoritism and its effects on your children.

Be aware. Since we are often unaware of the ways we may be favoring some kids over others, call upon the insight of others. Ask your spouse if he/she sees any evidence of you showing favoritism, and help your spouse be aware by sharing your insights. Ask your close friends if they see you playing favorites in any way. If your children are mature enough for such a conversation, ask them to talk to you about any feelings of being slighted. Admit to them that you're not perfect but that you love them equally and try to show it in what you do. Be careful, however, not to plant any seeds that aren't already there. Kids are smart enough to play the "you love Bobby more than me" card if they think it will help them control you.

Track the tangibles. Recognizing that much of the favoritism our kids may feel is subjective, it is still wise to be alert to what we do and say that may show favoritism. Compare the time you spend with your children. Listen to yourself as you speak to them. Do you compliment them all? Do you correct them for the same misbehaviors? Monitor your feelings toward your kids. Do you need to admit to yourself that you feel differently toward one child? Try to identify why. Compare what you do and what you give to your children. Are all these things generally equal?

Focus on who they are. The more you focus on each child's individual uniqueness and gifts, the more ammunition you will have to lavish each one with praise and compliments. Favoring children equally is not about reducing your positive feelings and actions toward one child but raising your appreciation for all of them. Children learn their value primarily from their parents. As you maintain focus on generously celebrating each child's gifts, uniqueness and accomplishments, they will be less likely to notice any momentary lapses in your efforts to treat them equally.

CONSIDER AND RESPOND

1. When you were a child, would you say that you were more favored, less favored or equally favored in comparison to your siblings? How did your parents show a disparity in favoritism, if at all?

2. Have you ever considered that you might be showing favoritism among your children? In which of the four ways mentioned in this chapter might you have fallen into the favoritism trap?

3. Ask your spouse to tell you honestly if he or she feels you are showing favoritism in some way. Discuss ways you can minimize favoritism.

4

Hey, Dummy!

Five-year-old Brianna (not her real name) was a student in our Children's Music Academy. Since we require a parent or grandparent to be involved with each child, Brianna's father came with her to the weekly classes. In most cases, working together in music class is a great way for a parent and child to bond. But it was the opposite for this father and daughter, and Dad was clearly the cause of this bad situation.

Instead of encouraging and helping his little girl, this father was critical, demanding and verbally abusive. If Brianna's hand was in the wrong position, Dad would slap the keyboard and blaze, "You know where to put your hand!" When Brianna suffered a momentary lapse in attention, he was all over her. "What's the matter with you? Why can't you focus?" And he wasn't quiet about it. The other students and parents heard everything. Dad even criticized the teacher in front of everybody. The atmosphere in the classroom was tense, and the teacher was afraid of confronting the father for fear of what he might do.

This went on week after week. In the middle of it all was poor little Brianna, degraded and humiliated in front of everyone by the

most important man in her life, the man who should have been her
champion and greatest fan.

I met a number of parents like Brianna's father over my years of
youth ministry. They have a problem showing proper respect for
people, including their children. The words and actions of
Brianna's dad communicated a devastating message to his daughter: You're not good enough, and I don't care who knows it. And
while Brianna responded in fear then, the seeds of long-term pain,
anger and potentially harmful behavior were sown.

ANGER GENERATOR 4:
TREATING YOUR CHILDREN WITH DISRESPECT

How many times have you been at the mall or a restaurant or a Little League game and heard parents verbally berate their children?
Many times during my youth work I was shocked by parents who
talked down to their teenagers and demeaned them in front of
their friends. I also recall with embarrassment my own disrespectful words and actions toward my children as I tried occasionally to
exert my power and solidify my position of authority over them.

Disrespect means a lack of respect, of course. We demonstrate
proper respect for people by cherishing and protecting their worth,
their rights and their feelings. And we are disrespectful when we
ignore or demean the worth, rights and/or feelings of others. That's
what was going on with Brianna in the CMA classroom—and
likely at home as well. Instead of nurturing and encouraging her,
Brianna's father railed on her, openly questioning her worth, violating her right to be treated with kindness and understanding and
tromping all over her tender feelings.

Disrespect hurts, and pain leads to anger. In his insightful and
practical book *Make Anger Your Ally,* psychologist Dr. Neil Clark

Warren comments on the linkage between disrespectful treatment and the anger it generates: "Violations to self-esteem through insult and humiliation are perhaps the most powerful elicitors of anger that we know about. When your potency and status are threatened, you will almost automatically become angry." If you treat your children with disrespect, you can count on an angry response from them. It may simmer beneath the surface for some time, but eventually it will erupt in some manner.

WOUNDING WITH WORDS

Disrespect has mostly to do with how we speak to our children, even though our actions will reinforce our words. Perhaps I'm more sensitive than others, but some of the most painful experiences in my life have been emotional, not physical. The deep hurt came from words spoken by my parents and others—unkind, disrespectful words that slashed through my heart.

As a high school sophomore I played on the junior varsity basketball team. My coach left an impression on me, but it wasn't a good one. He was a yeller and a screamer. I still wince as I remember a game in which I made a bad pass on the court. The coach jumped up from the bench and yelled, "Cross, you're an idiot." I think everyone in the stands heard his tirade. Those words cut to my soul. I felt hurt, frustrated and fearful—all emotions that lead to anger. He never apologized for his outburst, and there is no doubt in my mind that his hurtful words affected my play adversely for the rest of the year.

The disrespecting words we unleash on our children, reinforced by actions, can insult, humiliate and wound them. Our kids and teens don't have the emotional resilience or strength to combat the harsh words directed at them. Think how difficult it is for adults to do so! I'm convinced that the greatest single determinant in the development of children's self-esteem is how parents communicate to them. Respect through our words can build them up, and disrespect will tear them down.

In his book *The Key to Your Child's Heart,* Gary Smalley states that our words, voice inflection and body language can either open or close our children's hearts. We must avoid closing their hearts through our disrespectful communication. In *The DNA of Parent-Teen Relationships,* Smalley and his son Greg list the top five "spirit closers" and the hurtful words that convey these negative messages.

1. **Don't let them think on their own.**
   - "That's the stupidest thing I've ever heard."
   - "You're too young to understand."
   - "Who asked you?"
   - "Please don't interrupt. Can't you see I'm trying to solve this problem?"

2. **Inhibit their freedom to speak their mind.**
   - "That's enough talking. Go play and let us be alone for a while!"
   - "Is there an end to this?"
   - "What you say is always so confusing!"

3. **Regard their feelings as unimportant.**
   - "Come on, that's just the way your brother is. Stop taking everything so personally."
   - "That shouldn't hurt your feelings. Why, when I was your age I got twice as much teasing as you get."
   - "If you're going to get upset every time we go over there, I'm just not going to take you again."

- "Movies like that are just make believe. Grow up! There's nothing to be afraid of."

4. **Avoid spending time with them.**
   - "I've got two days to finish this report, so no, I can't go see your play."
   - "See if your mother will take you. I don't have time for it."

5. **Disrespect their individuality.**
   - "I said, don't lock the bathroom. I may need in there to comb my hair."
   - "I'm your father. I know what is best for you."
   - "Don't be silly. They'll like your hairstyle."

I believe there are two critical areas where we may be vulnerable to showing disrespect in conversation with our kids.

First, be aware that the way we talk to our kids often reflects how we're doing in the other areas of life. If we're feeling pressure in our marriages, finances or work, that pressure may spark unkind words in conversation with our kids.

Second, talking disrespectfully to children can become a bad habit. We can fall into a pattern of speaking down to our kids. It becomes second nature and we don't even notice how we're treating them. They may be "only kids," but they are building their own self-concepts based on what they hear and feel from us. This is a bad habit that must be overcome.

ANGER MINIMIZER 4:
TREATING YOUR CHILDREN WITH RESPECT

Whenever Brianna misplayed notes during the music lesson, her dad came down on her. "Can't you get anything right? You're always messing up. Why can't you hit the right notes?" And his tone wasn't civil; it was full of anger. Fearful of what might happen if she made another mistake, Brianna haltingly tried to keep up. But every failure brought another outburst, and every outburst brought tears and shut down her heart.

How could this scene have been different? The vast majority of the parents and grandparents in our program treat their young musicians with respect. We hear them say things like, "You're doing great," "I'm so proud of you" and "I think you only missed a couple of notes. Do you want to try it again?" With this kind of approach Brianna would have sensed the respect, encouragement and hope that open a child's heart.

Respect has a lot to do with applying the Golden Rule at home: "So in everything, do to others what you would have them do to you, for this sums up the Law and the Prophets" (Matthew 7:12). It's pretty simple: If we don't want other people—including our children—disrespecting us, we must show respect to others—including our children. Ephesians 4:29 admonishes, "Do not let any unwholesome talk come out of your mouths, but only what is helpful for building others up according to their needs, that it may benefit those who listen." This is the way we want others to speak to us, so we must speak to others—including our children—the same way.

The key to reversing the anger generator of treating kids with disrespect is to develop a mindset of respect for our kids as persons. We must learn to recognize their value and uniqueness. The psalmist writes

> "Children are a gift from the LORD;
> they are a reward from him." (Psalm 127:3 NLT)

Think about God's many gifts to you: salvation, eternal life, peace of heart and mind, purpose in life and so on. We wouldn't think of treating these precious gifts with disrespect. Well, our children are in that same category—gifts from God. They deserve the same kind of respect.

In their book on parent-teen relationships, Gary and Greg Smalley talk about honoring our children. Their definition of honoring applies to young children as well as to teenagers: "Deciding to place high value, worth, and importance on another person by viewing him or her as a priceless gift and granting him or her position in our lives worthy of great respect."

Notice that the definition begins with *decide*. Honoring our kids is a choice that doesn't always come naturally. Honoring doesn't mean you give up your position as parent or give away any of your responsibilities to train and discipline them. Honoring is about highly valuing your children as you go about training and disciplining them.

The Smalleys suggest four ways to honor our teenagers, and I think they apply to all ages of children as well:

- Place your teenager in a highly respected position. . . .
- See your teenager as a priceless treasure. . . .
- Demonstrate honor in your actions. . . .
- Suspend judgment and add curiosity.

I would add another: Let your words reflect this mindset of honor and respect.

Parenting with Love and Logic by Foster Cline and Jim Fay is one of the best parenting books available. In their chapter titled "Setting Limits through Thinking Words," they distinguish between the "fighting words" and "thinking words" we use with our children. Fighting words are commanding words, such as "Pick up your room this minute, young lady!" Thinking words come more in the form of a question: "Honey, will you please pick up your room? I think it will make both of us very happy."

The chart below illustrates this tip.

THINKING WORDS AND FIGHTING WORDS

Observe the difference between some fighting and thinking words:

- Child says something loud and unkind to the parents:
  FIGHTING WORDS: "Don't you talk to me in that tone of voice!"
  THINKING WORDS: "You sound upset. I'll be glad to listen when your voice is as soft as mine is."

- Child is dawdling with her homework:
  FIGHTING WORDS: "You get to work on your studying."
  THINKING WORDS: "Feel free to join us for some television when your studying is done."

- Two kids are fighting:
  FIGHTING WORDS: "Be nice to each other. Quit fighting."
  THINKING WORDS: "You guys are welcome to come back as soon as you work that out."

- Child won't do his chores:
  FIGHTING WORDS: "I want that lawn cut, *now!*"
  THINKING WORDS: "I'll be taking you to your soccer game as soon as the lawn is cut."

Thinking words take more work on our part. It seems to be more natural for us to use fighting words with our kids. But thinking words help open up the spirit of our kids because they are more respectful. Fighting words tend to shut kids down. You can minimize anger in your communication by using thinking words.

As a parent, you are the greatest contributor to your children's sense of self-worth, and your messages to them carry enormous weight. What they receive from you goes deep into their souls and either contributes to or erodes positive self-worth. Sadly, once your disrespectful words, inflections and body language are delivered, they cannot be retracted. But you can decide now what your next words and actions will be. Choose to respect your children and honor them with your words. It will help fill your home with peace instead of anger.

CONSIDER AND RESPOND

1. Can you remember a time as a child when your parents intentionally or unintentionally treated you with disrespect? How did they communicate it to you? How did it make you feel?

2. Jot down some examples of fighting words you sometimes use with your children. Jot down some examples of thinking words you could use in these situations.

3. Identify one area where you have been communicating disrespect to your children and what you will do to begin to honor them.

5   A World Without Boundaries

During his late twenties, Danny made an appointment to see a counselor because he was frustrated with his life. He complained, "Things just aren't going my way." He wanted to know if it was his problem or "just the dummies I hang out with."

It didn't take long for the counselor to discover Danny's root issue. He had seen it countless times among clients in Danny's age bracket. It traced back to Danny's parents and how they had raised him. His mom and dad were products of the 1960s. They rebelled against authority then, and their opinion hadn't changed by the time Danny, their only child, was born. They might have verbalized their philosophy of parenting something like this: "We believe our son is intelligent"—which he was—"and can make his own decisions. We will provide the right environment for him and allow him to be guided by his instincts."

Growing up, Danny's "instincts" were suspect at best. The phrase his relatives and schoolmates used to describe him was "a terror." Danny bullied other kids and demanded his own way in every situation. One teacher predicted that he would be in prison by age sixteen. Danny was able to avoid that prediction, but only because he never got caught. As he grew older he refined his image somewhat. Instead of calling him a terror, people used words like *slick, narcissistic* and *self-absorbed* for Danny.

Danny had grown up without any boundaries, set free by his free-spirited parents to do whatever he wanted. Without any accountability or personal discipline, Danny was an angry, unhappy young man whose self-centeredness had alienated him from almost everybody.

Danny's problem is widespread among kids today in a permissive society where parents fail to provide adequate boundaries. Contrary to what many parents think, kids want and need reasonable but firm boundaries maintained by their parents. Leaving kids to their own instincts provokes them to anger.

ANGER GENERATOR 5:
FAILING TO PROVIDE ADEQUATE BOUNDARIES FOR YOUR CHILDREN

Charlie and the Chocolate Factory is the delightful children's book by Roald Dahl that has spawned two major movies since it was published in 1964. It tells the story of the owner of a chocolate factory, Willy Wonka, who sponsors a contest that will award five children a tour of his chocolate factory and a lifetime supply of chocolates. The contest captures the imagination of the entire world.

When the five winners finally emerge, little Charlie Bucket from a very poor family is clearly the most normal. The other four are stark examples of children who grew up with few or no boundaries in certain areas of their young lives.

Augustus Gloop is a nine-year-old boy with no boundaries when it comes to eating. His huge size confirms his addiction to food. Veruca Salt is the victim of greed with no boundaries. She has very wealthy parents and demands that they buy her anything she wants—which they do. Violet Beauregarde's life is centered on chewing gum. She says she can't do without it. When she won the contest to visit Willie Wonka's factory, she was working on the same piece of gum that she had been chewing for three months. Mike Teavee has no boundaries when it comes to television. He watches it day and night.

Dahl's story is fiction, of course, but just change the names and the circumstances and it would describe any number of kids today. These are the kids all around us who are living without parental boundaries and paying a dear price for it. Without boundaries, kids go with their gut; there are no restrictions. It's all about meeting their desires, so it's no holds barred, do whatever you want, whatever meets your need. It's moral relativism in disguise.

Parental boundaries, like the borders of a country, are all about providing safety and security for our children. As I write this chapter, a debate rages about the security of our national borders. The issue is keeping us safe from terrorists intending to unleash another 9/11, so we are deeply concerned about the strength of our borders.

We show the same concern for safety and security when we erect fences or walls around our property, especially when our kids are young. We want them to be safe from the possible dangers outside these boundaries—harmful animals, wandering away and getting lost, etc. Similarly, proper behavioral boundaries for our kids will help keep them secure and safe.

Without boundaries, children feel vulnerable, unprotected and unloved. This anxiety and inner pain can erupt into anger, which may be expressed in a number of unhealthy ways, such as

- Unacceptable behavior, often in the extreme

- Greater susceptibility to peer pressure
- Disrespect for authority
- Inability to think for themselves
- Inappropriate motivations in life
- Tendency to blame others for mistakes
- Lack of personal discipline
- Inclination toward codependency
- Difficulty in making decisions
- Low self-esteem

What does a home where boundaries are insufficient look like? Here are a few scenarios that illustrate little or no parental guidance and protection:

- Kids are allowed to eat whatever and whenever they want, determine their own bedtimes, complain their way out of doctor and dentist appointments, etc.
- Kids can watch any TV programs and movies they want, surf the Internet without supervision, take courses that are easy and fun instead of those that will help them fulfill their potential, complain their way out of music lessons, etc.
- Kids are allowed to run free without parents knowing—or concerned about—who they're with, where they're going and what they're doing.
- Parents leave the Christian education of their kids to the church, school or the child's own resources.

WHY DO KIDS NEED BOUNDARIES?

In the process of raising two daughters and a foster son, there were a number of things Jan and I never had to teach. For example, we never had to teach our kids to snarl a defiant "No!" when they were instructed to do something they didn't want to do. They didn't need any coaching from us to know how to snatch a toy away from a playmate and announce, "Mine!" We never had to teach our kids to do the wrong things; those traits were inborn and started becoming visible even before they could talk. We had to teach them not to do the wrong things and to do right things.

Why? Original sin. The Bible tells us that Adam and Eve, our first parents, sinned, and this trait has been passed down to every human being (see Romans 5:19). We all come into life with a sinful nature. Just like you, your sweet, angelic-looking newborns were hardwired to do wrong instead of right. They weren't born with any boundaries; they must be protected from wrong and taught to do right. This task belongs to the parents.

The good news of the gospel is that Jesus came to provide forgiveness for our sin and give us a new nature, one that seeks to please God and do what is right instead of living only for ourselves (see Romans 5:19). But the old nature doesn't let go of us easily, and parents and children alike need boundaries to help us stay on the right path.

Many kids don't admit that they want or need boundaries in their lives. But the unspoken yearning for parental intervention is still there. In his book *The Seven Cries of Today's Teens*, Timothy Smith reviews the results of a Gallup Institute youth survey and reveals what kids are crying out for in today's culture. Each of the seven cries below is followed by the percentage of youth surveyed that identified with it personally.

The Cry	Percentage
1. The need to be trusted	92.7
2. The need to be understood and loved	92.2
3. The need to feel safe and secure where I live and go to school	92.1
4. The need to believe that life is meaningful and has purpose	91.6
5. The need to be listened to, to be heard	91.5
6. The need to be appreciated and valued	88.2
7. The need to be supported in my efforts	87.4

I believe the seven cries listed above reflect the security and self-esteem kids want. Without boundaries, they are frustrated because they are left on their own to figure out life. They don't experience the security that boundaries provide. I believe parents can answer these cries as they maintain loving boundaries.

ANGER MINIMIZER 5:
PROVIDING LOVING BOUNDARIES FOR YOUR CHILDREN

The boundaries you set for your children will come from your values and beliefs. For those of us who are Christians, these values and beliefs are rooted in God's Word because the Bible contains God's boundaries for us, his children. As we establish behavioral boundaries for our kids, they should derive from the boundaries in Scripture that keep us safe and secure, the boundaries that we are committed to live within.

Your core values must apply equally to you and your children.

In other words, don't set a boundary for your children that you ignore yourself. The boundaries you set for them should already be in place and visible in your life. For example, if one of the boundaries you set for them is eating healthy, nutritious foods, you must be eating the same way.

Boundaries will change as your children grow older, allowing them more freedom to set their own boundaries, which is a characteristic of adulthood. The boundaries you manage for them now will help them in the process of transitioning to setting and managing their own boundaries.

My wife was very good at setting boundaries about what our girls could eat. We are fairly health conscious, and Jan felt strongly about holding a limit on the amount of candy, soft drinks and snack foods our kids could eat. We didn't hold to total abstinence from sweets, but we set some boundaries. I'm sure our girls did their share of "sneaking," but now as adults they are very aware of putting the right foods into their bodies. We followed the Proverbs 22:6 approach to setting boundaries:

> Train a child in the way he should go,
>   and when he is old he will not turn from it.

The following questions will help you identify some of the boundaries you already have in place for your children and determine where you may need to establish new boundaries.

Boundaries for physical protection and safety

- What guidelines do you have for what your kids are allowed to eat and drink?
- How do you make sure they get the rest they need?

- What boundaries are in place for use of alcohol and illegal drugs?
- How do you guide your children in the area of personal cleanliness? Cleanliness of their rooms, clothes and other possessions?
- How do you monitor their need for physical activity through play, competitive sports activities and camps, etc.?

Boundaries for relational protection and safety

- What guidelines need to be in place to protect your children from the negative influence of classmates, peers and adults in their lives?
- How are you helping your child understand what true friendship is?
- Are your children allowed to respectfully question your guidelines and judgments? Under what terms?
- How are you helping your children act and speak with respect in relating to peers and adults?

Boundaries for spiritual protection and safety

- What guidelines do you have for your children's involvement in Sunday school, church services, youth group meetings and activities and church-sponsored retreats and camps?
- How are you assisting them in developing their own personal relationship with God and his Word?
- What guidelines do you provide to help your kids mature in biblical virtues such as selfless love for others, truthfulness, honesty, integrity, etc.?
- How are you helping them develop good stewardship over their time, money and abilities?

Boundaries for intellectual and emotional protection and safety

- What guidelines do you employ to help your children complete their schoolwork, select courses and majors, plan for college or a career?

- How do you feel about requiring or urging your children to consider intellectual pursuits outside their schoolwork (reading, visiting museums, taking music lessons and/or attending concerts, etc.)?

- How do you monitor your child's involvement with entertainment media such as television, movies/DVDs, music, computer/video games, Internet games and chat rooms, etc.?

Sorting through these many categories and setting boundaries may feel a bit overwhelming. But you have probably already established some boundaries in many of these areas, so your task is to evaluate where you are, refine what you are already doing and add new boundaries where necessary.

TIPS FOR SETTING BOUNDARIES

As you evaluate where you are and consider where you want to go, let me stress that the guidelines you implement should reflect the value system you personally embrace and endeavor to practice. The "do what I say, not what I do" approach will only fuel your children's anger.

Here are a number of helpful suggestions for setting boundaries.

Plan boundaries well. Many parental boundaries are not well thought out. They are often pontificated in the heat of the moment: "I'm so tired of your messy room; from now on you will clean it every morning before breakfast!" Boundaries established out of frustration or anger will often be overblown, unclear, too harsh and unachievable.

Communicate boundaries in the right spirit. Here are a couple of ways of communicating the same guideline. Which do you think will produce the best effect?

1. "I'm sick and tired of the way you have been talking to me, so I'm laying down the law. In the future, you will address me as 'father' or 'sir.' And if you cross over the line, I will ground you. Do you understand?"

2. "I'm not happy about how you have been talking to me recently. I want to be treated the same way you want to be treated. Please speak respectfully both in your words and tone of voice. If your speech isn't corrected, I will establish the appropriate discipline."

The first approach sounds more like a drill sergeant trying to whip his recruit into line. It's authoritative, disrespectful and controlling. The second is right-spirited, establishing a boundary without disrespecting or demeaning the child.

Make boundaries as positive as possible. Talk about the "why" for boundaries—the benefits of living within them. And whenever you talk about the discipline or punishment for violating a boundary, also talk about the rewards for not violating it.

Talk with your children to make sure your boundaries are clear. Spend all the time necessary to clarify the boundaries and respond to their questions and comments. For younger children, use simple terms and appropriate illustrations. Sincerely asking your kids if the boundaries are clear helps build their self-respect, especially as you use appropriate terms and a respectful tone of voice.

Be consistent. I'm not suggesting that your boundaries never budge, because boundary changes will be necessary as kids grow older and situations change. But arbitrary boundaries that change on a whim do not provide the security your kids need. If bedtime on school nights is set at 9:00 p.m., then you need to maintain that boundary consistently, with occasional exceptions for special occasions. Generally speaking, you should not change boundaries in response to threats, tears, pleadings, promises or begging from kids who feel mistreated. Use these occasions to sit down with them and calmly discuss the "whys and wherefores" of your boundaries. If you find that changes are necessary, you can make them based on mutual agreement instead of demands.

Tailor boundaries to each child. Your kids have different personalities and temperaments, so your boundaries for them should take these differences into account. For example, one child may need a boundary for keeping her room clean, but another may be a born neat freak and not need such a stated boundary.

Talk about your own boundaries. Your kids need to know that you live within certain boundaries just as you are asking them to do. Talk about the boundaries your parents set for you as a child. Talk about the boundaries you have set for yourself as an adult and why you live within them. And be honest about your own struggle to live within boundaries.

AGE DIFFERENCES AND BOUNDARIES

Boundaries must be administered differently depending on the ages of your children. In their terrific book *Boundaries with Kids*, Drs. Henry Cloud and John Townsend group boundary guidelines according to five age categories.

- *Birth to 12 months:* Boundaries should be minimal because babies can't tolerate much frustration. Concentrate on love and nurture.

- *One to three years:* Toddlers begin to understand the meaning of "no" and the consequences of their actions, but they don't yet understand the logic behind boundaries.

- *Three to five years:* They are better able to understand the reasons for being responsible and the consequences for not doing so. They are learning how to treat friends, respond to authority, and do chores.

- *Six to eleven years:* They are more aware of the outside world and their choices. They understand that violating boundaries may mean limiting activities, friends, etc.

- *Twelve to eighteen years:* This is a time of "de-parenting" as parental control gives way to influence. A child's freedom comes from handling responsibility well, not as a gift because of age.

In general, boundaries should be more restrictive when children are younger and gradually loosen up as the children grow older. As kids learn to handle responsibility they should earn greater measures of freedom. Unfortunately, many parents seem to do it backwards. Little kids are allowed a wide berth for misbehavior because their parents think it's cute or they don't want to stifle free expression. But when the kids reach the teens and really start spreading their wings, these parents suddenly clamp down in order to protect them from a "terrible world out there." This usually provokes a storm of anger and rebellion you wouldn't wish on your worst enemy.

As you already know, this subject of boundaries is difficult and has far-reaching consequences both for good and bad. It's one of those parts of parenting where you will need to give yourself lots of grace. You will fail. You will regret some of your decisions. But don't get down on yourself. Hopefully the thoughts and suggestions in this chapter will give you the hope and motivation to learn and improve as time goes by.

CONSIDER AND RESPOND

1. When you were growing up, what boundaries in your life proved to be the most beneficial to you? Which boundaries did you fail to understand when you were growing up?

2. Which of your top values are most clearly reflected in the boundaries already in place for your children? Which of your values seem to be missing or weakly represented in your boundaries?

3. What boundaries for your children do you need to establish or strengthen after reading this chapter? Which categories of boundaries are in need of your primary attention: physical, spiritual, relational or intellectual/emotional?

6   Crime and Punishment

As I write this chapter, I'm sitting in a Barnes & Noble bookstore near my home. Just a few feet away from me is a young mother and her son, who is about three years old. For the last several minutes, the little guy has been running wildly up and down the aisles while his mother searches for the book she wants. Every few seconds he yells out in a demanding tone, "Mama, come here!" Mama searches on without responding, so Junior keeps running and yelling to her using his "outside voice." Except he's not outside; he's in Barnes & Noble where people like me should be able to read, study or write in relative peace and quiet. I can't even think straight with Junior going off, and I see the same consternation on the faces of others nearby. But Mama seems oblivious to the disturbance her little darling is causing.

The irony hits me: I'm trying to write a chapter on the topic of parental discipline in the presence of a mother who acts like she's never heard of the concept and a little boy who is clear evidence of the allegation.

Discipline is the ongoing process of helping our children live within the behavioral boundaries we set for their well-being and correcting them when they violate those boundaries. I'm talking about appropriate consequences that underscore for the child the importance of boundaries and encourage him or her not to violate them. The purpose of discipline is to positively influence future behavior.

While conducting focus groups and surveys with young people in preparation for writing this book, no topic elicited more reaction than discipline. Some kids appreciated being disciplined; some did not. Some said they understood why discipline was necessary; others had no clue. But all the kids I interviewed had an opinion because all had firsthand experience with discipline or the lack of it in their homes. And for many of them their experience with discipline was a source of anger.

ANGER GENERATOR 6:
DISCIPLINING YOUR CHILDREN INAPPROPRIATELY

Parental discipline is a source of childhood anger because parents are imperfect and their discipline often reflects it. This reality came out in my interviews with kids as they expressed the problems they have with the discipline of their parents. Here's a summary of what they said to me:

- "We don't like being disciplined unfairly." They were referring to those times when "the sentence didn't fit the crime" or they were disciplined differently from their siblings or the boundaries kept changing. One teenager said, "I understand the correction but not how I was corrected."

- "We don't like being disciplined out of anger." They understood that their parents get angry at misbehavior, and they were OK with that. But they didn't want their parents to discipline them while they were angry or because they were angry.

- "We don't like being disciplined when the rules are not explained ahead of time." This complaint is more valid with older children who are able to comprehend the rules. "Because I said so" may work with very small children, but older kids and teens need to know in advance the rationale for boundaries.

- "We don't like being unable to express our opinion about discipline." Kids felt that, when it came to being disciplined, their parents' attitude was "It's my way or the highway." They felt it was unfair that they were not given a chance to tell their side of the story.

The word *discipline* is a cousin to the word *disciple*, meaning "a learner." The goal of disciplining children is to help them learn safe, healthy, productive and socially acceptable behavior. When our discipline is inadequate or inappropriate to the child or situation, the good lessons of discipline are blocked by the hurt and anger we provoke in our children. Inappropriate discipline usually causes more harm than good.

I believe there are two general ways parents provoke their children to anger with inappropriate discipline. First, they fail to administer discipline when it is needed. For example, Dad sets an 11:00 p.m. curfew for his teenaged son on Friday and Saturday nights. But when the kid comes in a 12:15 a.m. simply because he didn't want to come home early, Dad does nothing. The boundary is useless without an appropriate response when it is violated. Whenever they violate clear parental boundaries for their safety and receive no consequences, kids wonder if their parents really care, and this confusion and hurt can grow into anger.

Second, parental discipline is inappropriate and harmful to kids when it is administered incorrectly. This is what the kids in my fo-

cus groups shared with me: minor violations receive major penal-
ties, major violations are glossed over, boundaries and their consequences keep changing, discipline is administered in anger, and so
on. When discipline is unfair, anger may be the result.

ANGER MINIMIZER 6:
DISCIPLINING YOUR CHILDREN APPROPRIATELY

How can we discipline our kids appropriately and minimize their
anger? Here are six key principles that will help you bring your parental discipline into good balance.

Kids need discipline. If your children always lived within the
boundaries you set for their safety and security, they wouldn't need
the correction of your discipline. Some kids do much better than
others, but nobody's perfect, so parental discipline will always be
needed. You must continually remind yourself that appropriate
discipline is good for your child. In your loving acts of disciplining
them, you are helping them for the future.

Understand the difference between discipline and punishment.
The difference has to do with motives. The motive of punishment
is to make sure the child experiences pain for stepping over the line.
Discipline, while it usually involves some kind of pain (a swat, being grounded, privileges withheld, etc.) is motivated by correcting
and improving behavior. Punishment can often be administered in
anger, while discipline is more controlled and measured.

*Understand the transition between restrictive and permissive
discipline.* In the previous chapter I mentioned that boundaries
should be more restrictive when children are younger and gradually loosen up as they mature and become more responsible. The
same is true for discipline. During early childhood, the consequences for violating boundaries must be swift and sure so your

kids learn to respect those boundaries. Don't "chicken out" because your child is cute and innocent and you hate making her unhappy with your correction. Ten years from now she may not be quite as cherubic as she severely tests your boundaries. If you wait until then to tighten down the screws, it won't work, and you may provoke a big explosion of anger.

I'm concerned about this little tyke bouncing off the walls of the bookstore as I work. Mama either hasn't established a clear boundary for how he should behave in public or she is unwilling to make him toe the line. When will his misbehavior over the next several years push her to the boiling point, and what will she do to lay down the law? It could get ugly.

Being a disciplining parent requires courage and mental toughness. You've got to hang in there even when you're tired and don't want to bother with the correction and even when those big tears of remorse trigger your deepest sympathy. As you begin with a loving but restrictive environment and gradually loosen up, you will find that your teenagers will be equipped for making good decisions and your discipline at that stage will be easier.

Plan your discipline ahead of time whenever possible. You can't possibly anticipate all the different ways your children will violate the boundaries you have set for their behavior. But you should have a general idea of how you will respond before the more common violations occur—and let your kids know in advance what to expect. For example, you may say that failing to treat toys with proper care (leaving them out in the yard overnight, throwing them, etc.) will result in restricted use of toys or that violating the daily time limit for computer games will mean no computer play time for a week.

Predetermining your discipline plan and making it known to

your kids has several benefits. When a child knows the consequences ahead of time, he must take responsibility for his actions. It also eliminates any arguments with the child about what the consequences should be, reducing your stress level in the process. And predetermined discipline lessens the chance of you flying off the handle and reacting out of anger.

Follow through. All the planning and announcing of boundaries and consequences is worthless if you don't follow through with the discipline when the time comes. You may be busy, tired, stressed or otherwise not in the mood to deal with the situation when it occurs. But if you don't follow through, your kids may not learn the valuable lessons they need to learn. On some occasions you may have to delay dealing with a boundary violation because you are on your way to work or otherwise committed. But don't let the discipline slide. When the child learns that the consequences are unavoidable, it will motivate him to think seriously before stepping over the line.

Gradually hand the control of your children's lives over to them. The goal of parental discipline is to help our kids establish and live within their own boundaries. Discipline is not about maintaining a firm grip of control over our kids; it's about exerting only as much control as we need to while allowing them to control what they can. In *Parenting with Love & Logic,* Foster Cline and Jim Fay state about parental control, "The more we give away, the more we gain. . . . In the battle for control, we should never take any more than we absolutely must have; we must cut our kids in on the action."

While it is possible to give our children too much control, most parents err on the side of not allowing them enough control. Handing over control means allowing our children more choices in the process of staying within boundaries. Summarizing the work of psychologist Sylvia B. Rimm, Ph.D., Cline and Fay write, "Children who grow up with parents who dole out control in increasing amounts are usually satisfied with the level of control. It's always more than it used to be."

Gradually handing over more control to our children and giving them more choices is so important to maintaining safe boundaries for them. Dr. Rimm pictures it as a V, which she calls "the V of love." (See the chart on page 78.) Cline and Fay write, "The sides of the 'V' represent firm limits within which the child may make decisions and live with the consequences. The bottom of the 'V' represents birth . . . while the top represents the time when the child leaves home for adult life." Childhood and youth become the gradually liberating experience of earning greater control and more choices concerning their own lives, thus equipping them for adulthood.

Cline and Fay go on to explain why giving kids more choices in their behavior works.

- Choices make a child think. They are in charge of their decision. . . .
- Choices give opportunities for making mistakes and learning from consequences. . . .
- Choices prevent control battles between parents and children. . . .
- By giving choices, children know that we trust them.

A CASE STUDY IN CONTROL AND CHOICES

Six-year-old Marty sits with his parents in a booth at a fast food restaurant. Mom and Dad have finished their meals and are ready to go shopping. But Marty is blowing bubbles through his straw, playing airplane with his French fries and barely nibbling at his hamburger.

THE "V" OF LOVE

In the "V" of Love, the limits we set down for our kids' behavior are ever-expanding, offering more and more freedom as the years go by. Unfortunately, many parents do the opposite (the inverted "V"). They grant many privileges when the children are young and then find themselves taking control away from their kids. The result is unhappy children.

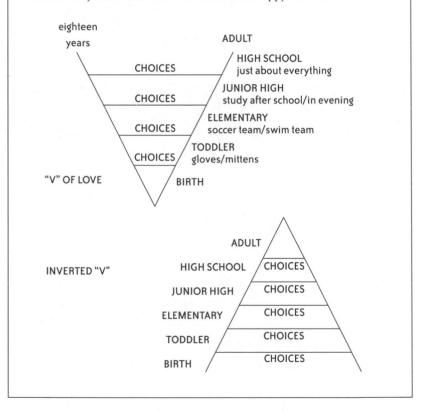

Mom says with agitation, "Hurry up and eat. We've got shopping to do." Marty responds by buzzing his burger with a fry. Next Mom grabs the burger and tries to feed it to Marty. He clamps his jaw shut.

Next Mom threatens to go shopping without Marty and leave

him there. Marty picks up the burger as if thinking about complying. Then the corners of his mouth tighten into a curt, self-satisfied smile. Dad sees it and jumps out of the booth. "OK, that's it! We're going shopping without you, and do you know what's going to happen to you, buddy? Cops are going to come and get you!"

Marty's hamburger flops down on the table. He has totally controlled his parents without saying a word. The last thing he is worried about is being picked up by the cops.

Marty's parents blew it entirely in trying to make him eat. Had they offered him choices instead of making demands, taking only as much control as they absolutely needed, they would have been able to put Marty in control on their terms. Here's how.

A love-and-logic parent would say with a smile on her face, "No problem, Marty. The car will be leaving in five minutes. There are two ways to leave with me: Hungry is one way; not hungry is the other."

This gives the parent as much control as he needs. He doesn't need to control whether the burger goes down the child's throat in fact, he can't control that. But he can control when the car leaves.

By offering choices, the struggle is transferred inside Marty's head. Marty's too busy to argue; he's weighing his choices: hungry or not hungry. In the meantime, Dad and Mom have five minutes of welcome tranquility. They gain control by relinquishing control.

Many parents, after issuing the alternatives, would be tempted to harp and nag while the child is making up his mind. They would say things like, "Don't forget, my car is leaving in three minutes. If you don't eat that food you're going to be hungry." These sorts of reminders are putdowns. Cut the kid some slack. Marty's smart enough to remember the choices he's been given.

When the five minutes are up, Dad would then enforce the child's choice. He could use fighting words like, "You get in the car," but much better would be thinking words like, "My car is leaving now."

Marty might say, "But I'm not finished."

Once again Dad would offer Marty choices. "No problem, son. We're leaving now, and you can go under your own power or my power, either one"—followed by ten seconds for Marty to decide. The point Marty understands is that the car's departure doesn't depend on whether or not he's done eating. The car is leaving—period.

Assuming that Marty decides not to come with Dad willingly, Dad must pick him up and head for the door. It's important to note that there are always three choices. In this example, Marty can do it one way or the other. The third option is that the parent will decide if Marty fails to decide, which is what happened here.

A lot of parents are bothered by what comes next. Marty will probably leave kicking and screaming like a banshee. Everybody in the restaurant will be watching. Let them watch. Teaching a child responsibility is not a free ride. We must steel ourselves for resistance and opposition. There's a price we must pay.

To ensure that Marty has a learning experience from this incident, his mom and dad must remember one thing: to keep their mouths shut. Save the words for the happy times. The only time to reason with a child is when both parties are happy. Parents who discipline their child with their mouths moving strip the consequence of its value. Allow the consequences to do the teaching.

Carrying the kicking and screaming Marty out the restaurant door, Dad would then put him very gently in the car and drive off, all the while keeping mum about the incident. Before the evening is over, Marty will probably say something like, "I'm hungry."

When he does, Dad should stifle the temptation to get angry and say, "Sure you're hungry. I try to tell you these things but you never listen. That'll teach you to eat your hamburger in the restaurant." Such a response only engenders more antagonism in the child.

Dad should administer the consequences with a compassionate sadness. For example: "Oh, for sure, son. That's what happens to me when I miss my dinner. I'll bet you'll be anxious for breakfast. Don't worry. We'll cook a good one."

Without a doubt, Marty will learn more from this response than from anger and threats. Sorrow and consequences and an arm around his shoulder are powerful learning agents.

Screen legend Bette Davis is credited with saying, "If you've never been hated by your child, you've never been a parent." Her statement may be in the extreme, but there is some truth in it. You will never be perfect at administering discipline, so your occasional failures may make your kids angry. And even when your discipline is done well and in the right spirit they may still think you are their enemy instead of their friend. But you will get better at it with patience and practice, and as you grow in the ministry of parental discipline you will minimize the anger associated with it.

CONSIDER AND RESPOND

1. Review the six key principles for parental discipline in this chapter. Thinking back on your own childhood, which principles did your parents practice well? Which did they not practice well?

2. Which of these principles is most difficult for you to grasp or implement? Which is most difficult for your spouse?

3. Think through some of the common discipline situations you face with your children. What help did the principles and case study in this chapter provide for improving these situations? What will you do first?

7

Forcing Your Faith

Ted and Sandy are middle-class parents living in a nice home located where the city blends into the suburbs. Ted is an accountant in a small firm. Sandy runs a home-based craft business and spends time caring for her aging mother. They have three kids: Billy is fourteen, Heather is twelve, and Connie, who was something of a surprise, is three.

Ted and Sandy have always taken their kids to Sunday school and church with them. They have also nudged their kids into neighborhood Bible clubs, called Good News clubs. And as soon as Billy was old enough for the youth group, Ted and Sandy made sure he was there. Passing their faith on to their kids is very important to these parents.

But for Billy and Heather, interest in church, Bible clubs and spiritual things is going downhill fast. Heather whines and complains every time she's told to get ready for church. And Billy flat out refuses to go. Even the high-energy youth group has lost its luster for him. Ted and Sandy are worried about the older kids' lack of interest and the influence it may have on their three-year-old, who still loves Sunday school. They are holding a hard line and making the kids attend because they are afraid that if they don't, Billy and Heather may fall away from the faith.

Richard, age twenty-nine, is the youngest of six children. His father's involvement in business, missionary work and the military meant that the family lived all over the world. As a result Richard learned five languages while growing up.

Richard's dad and mom had a deep Christian faith. They made a commitment early in their marriage that they would actively pass on their faith to their children. They saw mealtimes as the perfect opportunity to "educate" their kids. It didn't matter what the kids had on their schedules or how they felt about it, nothing was allowed to interfere with family devotions around the dinner table. The evening meal was served and the Bible was drummed into them.

Richard shares his perspective on his parents' efforts to pass along their faith: "I have no doubt about my parents' good motives and sincerity. But they didn't understand that kids don't like religion forced on them. At some point the children have to come to faith on their own terms. My siblings and I resented our parents' faith for a long time because we saw it as something that stopped us from doing what we wanted to do. So we all walked away from God for several years. My older brother is still mad. It took me five years of rebellion before I came back."

It's only natural that parents want to share their deep beliefs with their kids in hopes that they will believe the same way. Our deepest desire is that our kids embrace a personal relationship with Jesus Christ because a truly purposeful life and their eternal destiny hinge on such a decision. The problem is that we are not raising robots or clones of ourselves. Our children are unique individuals with minds and souls of their own. We can lovingly explain what we believe about God and share what such a belief means to us. But pressuring our kids to adopt our faith may anger them and even push them in the opposite direction.

In my ministry to youth and families, I have talked to countless numbers of parents who wanted desperately to transfer their faith to their children without turning them off. I've heard their stories of success and their stories of tragedy. I've spent hours and hours with kids who are ticked off at their parents over this subject and have vowed never to follow the God they serve. In this chapter I want to help you defuse this anger in your kids by learning positive ways to share your faith at home.

ANGER GENERATOR 7:
IMPOSING YOUR FAITH ON YOUR CHILDREN

I believe there are three reasons behind the anger some kids feel when growing up in a home where Christian values are taught.

Kids resent being force-fed the faith. Let's admit it: We feel a sense of urgency about communicating our faith to our children while they are still with us. And in our urgency we wrongly try to force-feed them faith and salvation. Like Ted and Sandy, we make them to go to Sunday school, church and other "churchy" activities. We force them to act or dress a certain way because we go to church. We forbid them from participating in things their friends are doing because it isn't something our church would approve.

When kids feel forced to do something they don't want to do, especially as they enter the teenage years, they tend to get angry and dig in their heels. If we persist, they may even reject the very faith we are pressuring them to embrace.

Kids resent inconsistent examples. I'm talking about parents who don't walk the talk. If you say that your faith is important but you don't demonstrate that faith in your life, your kids will see through it and be turned off. They want to know that your faith is real, that it does what you say it does. They need to see a faith that makes a difference in how you live—in all of your life. If they don't see you practicing what you preach, then to them what you preach doesn't make sense. Their response is, "Your faith doesn't really work, so why should I embrace it? And please don't try and make me."

Kids resent rigidity. Some parents try to pass on their faith in an inflexible framework that doesn't allow challenge from their kids. When children are younger, they can accept rigid structure better. But as they grow older, "This is the way we do things in this family" becomes increasingly ineffective and provokes anger. Middle school and high school aged kids want to know why. They don't mind that you have strong beliefs; they just don't want them delivered in a package that says, "Do not question." Refusing to allow any discussion on the topic of faith may be interpreted by your kids as, "My arguments are weak, so I will not be put in a position where I have to defend them."

It is biblical to pass on our faith in our families. The apostle Paul celebrates Timothy's faith, which apparently formed and flourished under the instruction of his mother and grandmother (see 2 Timothy 1:5). And Paul's instruction to the Ephesians about angering kids is followed immediately by these words: "Instead, bring them up in the training and instruction of the Lord" (Ephesians 6:4). We need to discover how to convey the discipline and instruction of the Lord in ways that are winsome and not pushy.

ANGER MINIMIZER 7:
SHARING YOUR FAITH WITHOUT FORCING IT

The faith of a child or an adult doesn't develop overnight. I believe there are three broad stages to embracing faith. You went through these stages and so must your children. If you work within these stages you are less likely to anger them by forcing your faith.

Stage One: Introducing the faith. Suppose someone says to you, "I've got a great financial system that guarantees millions of dollars in retirement income. Give me all your available cash and trust me that it will work." You have two big decisions to make. The first is whether you trust the person making the offer. The second is whether you trust the system he is offering. If the person is someone you know well and whose financial advice has an excellent track record, you may be interested. But if it's a marketer on the telephone with a slick spiel, you likely won't even listen to him.

In offering your faith to your kids, you have a great advantage because you are already someone they know, love and trust. You are not a stranger trying to sell them the Brooklyn Bridge. Your love and nurture over the years has earned their trust. As you seek to transfer your faith to them, they come predisposed to pay listen and buy in.

Stage Two: Examining the faith. If the person offering a "can't miss" financial opportunity is deemed trustworthy, you move on to your second big decision: Do you believe that the system he's offering will work for you? If you act on blind faith you will simply hand your money to your friend. But most people don't operate that way; they want to see how the system works and how it will work for them. So you will probably want to find out everything you can about the system before you commit to it. In the same way, since our kids already trust us, we need to allow them plenty of room to examine the claims of the Christian faith in their own lives without pressuring them.

Stage Three: Embracing the faith. In the process of examining your friend's financial opportunity, at some point you need to make a commitment to go ahead with it. You likely will not know everything there is to know about it, but you know enough to write the check, expressing your faith in your friend and in the opportunity he presents.

Your kids need the same opportunity. Give them the freedom to examine the faith freely, question its foundations and explore its possibilities, all within the warmth of your love, acceptance and nurture. This is the environment they need to make *your* faith *their* faith. But the choice must be theirs.

COMMUNICATE YOUR FAITH WITHOUT PRESSURE

The stages for embracing faith will give you a context for the following suggestions for communicating your faith to your children without pressure.

Be less direct as your children grow older. This idea parallels the V of love illustrated in chapter 6. Communicating your faith can be pointed and direct when your children are very young, but it should get less so as they grow older, allowing room for them to question and explore.

Young kids are like sponges. They drink in everything you say in terms of teaching. Their spirits are more open. They think you have all the answers. Now is the time to teach them all you can about your faith in ways they can understand. Read stories to your young children that convey God and faith. Give them examples of God's goodness in your everyday life. Make it pleasant and inviting; don't make it a chore.

As your children reach late childhood and develop greater reasoning skills, your teaching style should change. When they are younger you might say to them something like, "We believe the right way to act in this situation is . . ." But for older children who are learning to make their own decisions you might say, "Let me explain how I think we should act in this situation and why." The next step might be asking, "What do you think? Do you agree that we should act this way? Why or why not?"

One loving Christian mom who had given her kids plenty of room to explore and question was concerned about her teenaged daughter's faith. The girl wasn't showing much interest in spiritual things. Her mom asked in a nonthreatening tone, "If your life was a house, what rooms would Jesus be in?" The girl thought for a moment and said, "Probably the basement." Mom accepted her daughter's answer without judgment. She demonstrated her interest without preaching to her daughter, hoping it would leave the door open for deeper conversations in the future—which is indeed what happened.

The direct versus indirect approach was vividly illustrated to me during a class I took for graduate work. The professor blindfolded one student and then instructed a seeing student to direct him across the classroom through a maze of chairs with voice commands—turn left, take two steps forward, etc.—as the rest of the class watched. It took some time, but the guide eventually succeeded in directing his partner to the goal.

Next, the professor selected another pair of students and blindfolded one for the same exercise. This time, however, the guide was not allowed to give directions; he could only respond to the blindfolded student's questions. As you might expect, it took longer for this pair to complete the task, but they were successful also.

Then the professor asked the two guides to comment on their roles. The first guide said he felt in control and liked giving directions. The second guide said he felt frustrated and wanted to blurt out directions to help his partner. Then the professor asked the two who had been blindfolded, "If you were to come back into the room blindfolded *without* your leader, could you finish the maze by yourself?" The directed student didn't think he could do it, but the student who asked questions said, "Yeah, I think I would do fine by myself."

The exercise illustrates that people who live by directions tend to depend on directions. They don't have to think or question; they just do what they're told. That's why the first student didn't think he could complete the maze by himself. But people like the second student, who must find their way by thinking for themselves, questioning and exploring, are more independent and confident.

Teaching the faith to our children involves both processes. When they are young they need direction. But if we don't loosen up as they grow and allow them to seek and explore on their own, they won't feel confident finding faith on their own. Giving directions is easier for us and takes less time. But the goal is for our children to find faith by themselves. We must help them seek faith for themselves because we won't be around forever.

Be authentic. Kids doubt the authenticity of your faith when you act one way at church and another way in the car on the way home. If they don't see a connection between what you say and what you do, they won't be attracted to your faith. Being authentic means you are the same person at church and at home, among Christians and among non-Christians, when things are going well and when things are going poorly.

Being authentic also means that you're real about your imperfections. They know that you don't have it together all the time, so it's important that you are up-front about your failures and sin. I'm not talking about going over the sordid details for your kids. Just be honest enough to say you blow it and need God's forgiveness. You are not only being authentic, but you're teaching them how to handle failure, disappointment and sin.

Authenticity also welcomes hard questions from your kids about faith, even questions you don't know how to answer. More than once my daughters questioned my thinking about some aspect of my faith. It wasn't comfortable, but it did make me think and study and led me to change my mind on some issues. The goal of authenticity in these situations is not to prove we are right but to demonstrate that we are seeking the truth.

Show them the positive side of your faith. Many kids grow up seeing the Christian faith as negative—rules, commandments, prohibitions, no fun. They usually get this idea from their parents, who convey that the Christian faith is mostly about stuff you can't do, and a faith like that isn't very appealing to kids. There definitely are boundaries for our behavior in the Bible, but there is also an abundance of freedom and joy within those wide boundaries. You need to examine how your faith comes across to your children.

Do your kids see your faith as inviting or burdensome by the way you live it out? Do they see how your faith works to help you handle failure, deal with evil in the world, improve relationships with your spouse and others, help you make decisions, impact how you deal with money and materialism? Are the joy, adventure and fun of following Christ visible in your life? I'm not proposing that you try to make your faith look better than it is so your kids will buy into it. Just let them see it all just as it is.

Communicate your faith through structured teaching and through life experiences. There is a time for structured teaching for your children from outside your family, such as Sunday school and church, Bible clubs, vacation Bible school and other training offered by church or parachurch ministries. Structured teaching can also happen in the home as you read Christian books to your kids, watch and discuss videos, have family devotion times and so on. You should know that some families seem to flourish with teaching structure in the home and some do not. Richard's experience, from the beginning of this chapter, is an example of how family devotions forced on the kids can be a detriment to them embracing the faith. Be sensitive to what your kids can handle in regard to structured teaching in the home, especially as they grow older, and work within those parameters.

No matter how much structured teaching your kids receive, I firmly believe that your faith will come alive to them as they see and experience it in the context of everyday living. This has been God's plan all along, as revealed in Deuteronomy 6:4-7:

> Hear, O Israel: The LORD our God, the LORD is one. Love the LORD your God with all your heart and with all your soul and with all your strength. These commandments that I give you today will are to be upon your hearts. Impress them on your children. Talk about them when you sit at home and when you walk along the road, when you lie down and when you get up.

Learn to see common life experiences as effective teaching tools. Talk about what God is doing in your own life and prayers that he has answered during normal conversations around the dinner table, when driving in the car and so on. When the kids are hurting, pray for them using simple, conversational prayers. When you experience something beautiful or fun with your kids, verbalize your thanks to God in their hearing: "Thank you, God, for the beautiful flowers in our garden"; "Thank you, Lord, for protecting us from that reckless driver"; "God, you paint the most beautiful sunsets!"

Here's a hard thing to grasp, but it's true: When it comes to passing on your faith to your kids, you can do everything right and your kids may still reject it. This doesn't mean you are a bad parent. After all, you wouldn't call God a bad father, but his first two children, Adam and Eve, walked away from him anyway. Ultimately, your children are responsible before God for their own lives and what you lovingly share with them about God and salvation. They are free to embrace the faith and free to turn their backs on it.

But there is also good news. I have met literally hundreds of people who as children or youth rejected God but as adults came back to the faith of their parents. Don't give up sharing your faith and praying for your kids.

CONSIDER AND RESPOND

1. Did your parents actively share their faith with you when you were a child? What did they do right in this area? What could they have done better?

2. What warnings and tips from this chapter do you most need to implement as you seek to share your faith with your kids? Where will you start?

3. Consider sitting down with each of your older children and discussing any changes you plan to make in sharing your faith at home. If you need to apologize for forcing your faith on them, do so sincerely.

8

Who's the Parent?

My dad makes me mad because he expects me to act like his wife."

The comment was offered by a girl I'll call Jennifer while I was interviewing a small group of students for this book. I hesitated to respond to her statement because I wasn't sure where she was going with it. Finally I said, "Are you comfortable saying more?"

The pretty eighth grader nodded. "What I mean is that I'm expected to do the laundry, cook the meals and take care of my little brother while Mom and Dad are at work and whenever Mom is away. It's like I'm a slave in my own house, and my dad is the slave driver."

I expected Jennifer to puddle up with tears of sadness. But as she went on, her voice and body language revealed a growing anger that was centered on her dad as the authority in her home. Jennifer felt that her teenage years were being stolen from her. She wanted to have fun, be involved in school activities and go to the mall with her friends. But her responsibilities at home and pressure from her father to run the house like a second wife had prevented such experiences.

Jennifer's dilemma and the anger it produced in her is a growing problem among kids in our society. The two major contributing factors are our high standard of living and our high rate of divorce. In a large percentage of two-parent homes both parents must work in order make ends meet and achieve the American dream. This often means that the children in these homes, like Jennifer, are expected to carry the load of responsibilities usually relegated to adults. In single-parent homes the load can be even greater because of the double burden of responsibility on either the mom or the dad. Kids in this setting who are forced into shouldering parental responsibilities feel robbed of their childhood, and it makes them angry.

ANGER GENERATOR 8:
BURDENING YOUR CHILDREN WITH PARENTAL RESPONSIBILITIES

In any family there are kid-sized responsibilities and there are adult-sized responsibilities. Problems arise when kids are pushed into a variety of adult-sized tasks that they shouldn't have to handle. I can see several areas where this happens.

Major responsibility for adult chores. These tasks include preparing meals, doing the laundry, repairing the car, painting the house, maintaining the yard and so on. I believe that children should be increasingly involved in these and other chores as they grow older; it's how they grow into handling responsibility. But it is inappropriate to burden kids with adult-sized responsibility for these or other jobs.

For example, even preschool children can be taught to take plates from the table to the kitchen sink as part of after-dinner clean up. But it is unreasonable to hold a four-year-old responsible for cleaning the entire kitchen. Kids of all ages should be given increasing responsibility for straightening and cleaning their own rooms. But it is unreasonable and damaging to burden a kid with all the weekly housecleaning.

I've heard about situations in which the child is forced to do all the chores while the mother watches soap operas or runs around with her boyfriend or husband. More common, however, are parents who load their kids down with chores as "teaching opportunities" when in truth they just don't want to do the work themselves.

Adult childcare duties. One of the biggest pressures kids reported in my surveys was the burden of caring for their younger siblings. Even though some respondents undoubtedly exaggerated their "plight," teenagers complained that their little brothers or sisters were unfairly dumped on them. Some said that their parents knew the teens were always there as a last resort when they couldn't find another babysitter. And since many of them didn't get paid like an outside babysitter, they felt cheated and disrespected by their parents.

Adult emotional needs. When a parent's emotional needs are not being met by a spouse, they turn to other individuals. It could be a counselor, a same-sex friend or someone from the opposite sex, opening the door to an affair. Many kids say that one or both of their parents lean on them for emotional strength or comfort. A mother will lament to a son her difficulty in relating to or communicating with her husband—his dad. Or the parent may dump his or her problems on the child and ask for advice. I've had young people tell me with anger in their voices that being treated this way makes them feel very awkward. They don't know what to say, and they don't feel comfortable being pitted against the other parent.

An extreme version of emotional dependence is parents who look to their children or other children to meet their sexual needs. Not long ago a middle-aged woman in our city was arrested and charged with multiple crimes stemming from the weekly sex, booze and drug parties she sponsored for teenaged boys in her neighborhood. She explained that she was never popular with her classmates in high school, so the house parties, which she ran for a year, left her feeling like one of the gang. Tragically, some parents exploit their own children sexually.

Adult decision-making responsibilities. Some of the kids in my surveys said they got angry when their parents abdicated (they used the term *dumped*) their decision-making roles. For example:

- A father tells his child to answer the phone call he knows is for him and tell the caller, "My dad's not here."

- A dad is asked by his wife to take the trash barrels out to the curb, and then he makes his son do it instead.

- A busy mom demands that her eight-year-old daughter take care of her baby brother, who has just fallen and skinned his knee.

- A mom doesn't like the next-door neighbor, so she sends one of the kids over whenever she needs to borrow something.

One way we abdicate decisions is by letting kids get away with behaviors outside our boundaries for them. If they step over the boundary of their curfew, for example, and we do nothing about it, we have in effect said the decision about when they get home is up to them. They are often not ready emotionally to handle that decision and may even be hurt and angry that you let them do what they want.

As children get older, I think it is good to ask them for their input on the decisions you need to make, especially those that directly impact them. Both of my daughters seemed honored when, during their teenage years, I asked for their opinions on some decisions I had to make. For example, I once asked one of our girls for her opinion on something I should buy for the home. She lived there too, so I thought it was only right to ask her. Not only did she feel honored by my request, but she gave great advice!

Asking for your kids' advice or opinion is healthy, but abdicating the responsibility for major decisions burdens them with more than they can handle, and it makes them angry.

ANGER MINIMIZER 8:
GIVING YOUR CHILDREN KID-SIZED RESPONSIBILITIES

Let me suggest four proactive steps you can take to minimize the anger your kids experience when they are over-burdened with adult responsibilities.

Examine your motives for the responsibilities you place on them. We need to ask ourselves why we give our children certain tasks and responsibilities where inappropriate role reversal is a possibility. And whenever we discover that our motives are self-centered instead of seeking the best for our kids and the family, we need to deal with that selfishness.

Most kids understand having to accept responsibility for their part within the family unit. What they resent and what makes them angry is when they think their parents are taking advantage of them for personal reasons or "pulling a power trip" in order to brandish their authority.

Why do we sometimes do such things? Parenting is a tough job. You are busy providing for the family. There are many outside pressures you can't control. The culture seems to be working against you and your children. You likely had little training in how to parent selflessly. Often the demands we make on our children are the result of reacting to our situations instead of following a well thought through plan for parenting.

But none of these legitimate influences should stop you from ex-amining your motives and dealing with the self-centeredness you find. I can tell you from my own experience and from observation of other parents that a child's anger in this area is often justified. Most of the time it is the parent, not the child, who initiates role reversal. Kids don't want to do the job of a parent. Life is tough enough for them already. Look through the four specific anger gen-erators mentioned above and make sure you are not triggering role reversal for the wrong reasons.

Examine your own family background. We tend either to repeat patterns from our upbringing or react against them. So if you grew up in a home where adult responsibilities were unfairly foisted on you, you may find yourself repeating that pattern with your own kids or swinging the other direction and withholding responsibil-ity from them. For example, if you had to do all the housecleaning as a young person, you may make the same demand on your kids or you may do everything yourself so they don't feel the pain you felt. You may need to come to terms with your own childhood hurt and anger in order to deal fairly with your kids.

Make sure your own needs are being met. If you find that you are leaning on your kids to do things you should be doing or to meet your emotional needs, you need to step up to those responsibili-ties. You cannot expect your children to parent you or meet your needs. They are not responsible for your comfort or happiness. The apostle Paul wrote, "When I was a child, I used to speak like a child, think like a child, reason like a child; when I became a man, I did away with childish things" (1 Corinthians 13:11 NASB). Children depend on others to meet their needs; adults put away childish ways and take responsibility for their own needs.

Check your self-esteem. Pushing adult responsibilities onto your children may be the result of doubting your own worth, so you expect things of them that you would never expect from yourself. You may need to bolster your self-esteem by realizing who you are as God's child.

If you and your children live long enough, there likely will come a time when the roles will be reversed. You take care of them now; they will take care of you later. This may have already happened in your relationship with your parents. Most people reach an age when their ability to take care of themselves begins to diminish. At some point the children take responsibility for their parents, even to meeting their basic needs. You may be "parenting" your own parents now or in the future, and some day your kids may be parenting you.

But until then, you need to let your kids be kids and enjoy it. Teach them responsibility, but don't weigh them down with the responsibilities of adulthood until they have reached that stage. If you let them grow into adult responsibilities, you will have the joy of seeing them mature in joy and peace and not in anger.

CONSIDER AND RESPOND

1. Can you identify a role reversal situation in your family when you were a child? How did your parents tend to push their responsibilities onto you or a sibling? How did you feel about the situation? How did you respond?

2. Do you see any areas in your present family life where you may be burdening any of your children with responsibilities too great for them? How will you change the situation?

3. Ask your children if they feel any pressure from you in the area of responsibilities. What can you and your spouse do to prevent role reversal from happening with your children?

9   The Two-Headed Monster

Kim found her eleven-year-old daughter, Emily, in the utility room Saturday morning sorting dirty laundry. "Are you still planning to go to the mall with Aly this afternoon?" Kim asked.

Emily frowned. "Dad said no."

"Why?"

"Because Aly's mom can't stay with us, and Dad doesn't want us going without adult supervision."

Kim laughed. "Doesn't he realize that there are security guards all over that mall on Saturday? You're perfectly safe there."

"That's what I told him, but he still said no."

Kim fished a twenty-dollar bill from the pocket of her jeans and handed it to Emily. "Well, I don't see anything wrong with it, so I say yes. You go on to the mall and have a good time. I'll explain everything to your dad."

Sixteen-year-old Nate nervously waited until his family was finished eating supper to share his news. "Mom and Dad, I've decided to enroll at State University after high school. They have a really good baseball program."

"That's terrific, Nate," Dad said, beaming. "I think you've got a

shot at pro ball, and State U will help get you there. I'll do everything I can to—"

"Wait a minute, Ron!" Mom interrupted, scowling at her husband. "I don't want Nate focusing on baseball. He needs to zero in
on academics, prepare for a career."

"I'm thinking about his career too, Leslie," Ron snapped. "And
I'd call $10 million a year playing baseball a pretty good career."
Then he added to Nate, "Wouldn't you, son?"

Leslie cut in before Nate could answer. "You both know that the
odds of Nate becoming a baseball superstar are a zillion to one. He
needs an education, Ron. I will not let you push him into being the
jock you want him to be."

"Pushing?" Ron steamed. "Isn't that what you're doing, pushing
our son into an education and career he may not even want? If it's
a pushing match you want, Leslie, you just wait to see who can
push harder, you or me."

These two scenarios represent the wide variety of family situations I encountered during my ministry with Youth for Christ. The
common denominator in these situations is parents—either married or divorced—who live in a degree of conflict with each other
over how to raise their children. As seen in the two vignettes, the
conflict may be subtle and behind-the-back or bitter and noisy. But
parents in conflict are pulling against each other instead of pulling
together, and that's not good for their kids.

I'm not saying that you will always be in agreement over how to
raise your kids. In fact, to paraphrase an old saying, if parents
never disagree about anything then one of them isn't necessary.
You are different persons with different backgrounds, experiences,
perspectives, insights and abilities. Count on it: You will disagree
from time to time over boundaries, discipline and other parenting

issues. But if you and your spouse—or ex-spouse—constantly clash over parenting style and decisions, especially in front of the children, it will take a heavy toll on your children. Conflict over parenting will dramatically limit the effectiveness of the other anger minimizers in this chapter. And the ultimate fallout from the two-headed monster of parents in conflict is insecurity, hurt and anger in the children.

ANGER GENERATOR 9:
CONFLICTING OVER PARENTING STYLE AND DECISIONS

As the story of Emily's mom and dad illustrates, one of the most common parental conflicts is over a child's boundaries and the consequences for violating those boundaries. One parent wants to hold a tight leash; the other prefers to give the kids more room. One is a strict disciplinarian; the other is a pushover or uses a sliding scale. These kinds of parents tend to operate independently, and the kids are caught in the middle. Though the kids may enjoy using their parents' conflict to their advantage, the lack of agreement provides a shaky, insecure foundation for them.

As the story of Nate's parents illustrates, parents may conflict because they have different agendas for their kids. Dad may be pushing math, science and shop classes while mom insists on English, history and music—or vice versa. One may lobby for a secular university but the other won't allow anything less than a solidly Christian school. The poor kid is like the rope in a tug-of-war. He can't win no matter which parent he sides with.

Parental conflict also results when parents compete for their children's favor and friendship by making the other parent look like the "bad guy." Some parents oppose each other in parenting as payback for being hurt by the other parent. Some parents end up in conflict when one of them—often the father—abdicates the training and disciplining role to the other. To his spouse he says, "You handle it; it's not my job." To the kids he says, "Your mom will do it when she gets home."

Let me repeat: All parents face these and other kinds of disagreements in how to raise their kids. But kids suffer when their parents fail to resolve these disagreements and allow them to build into ongoing conflict. Disillusionment, insecurity, hurt and anger happen to kids when parents do two things at the point of disagreement. First, they perpetuate the conflict instead of resolving it. Second, they air their clashes in front of the children instead of working through them privately.

ANGER MINIMIZER 9:
HARMONIZING OVER PARENTING STYLE AND DECISIONS

Jesus said, "A house divided against itself will fall" (Luke 11:17). He wasn't referring specifically to two parents in a home, but I believe the principle applies. Kids feel more secure and at peace when their parents live in harmony. If you want your kids to grow up feeling secure and at peace at home, you and your spouse or ex-spouse must work hard at building a harmonious relationship.

I want to share a number of important characteristics for harmony between parents in the midst of parenting challenges. I have arranged them into two categories. The first is for parents who are still married to each other and parenting together. The second is for parents who are separated or divorced but maintain shared custody of the children.

MARRIED PARENTS IN HARMONY

These first few paragraphs focus in on how to relate to each other when you are dealing with a disagreement that threatens to erupt into a conflict.

Address disagreements right away. If I were Emily's father and her mother just told me she had reversed my decision about Emily going to the mall, I would get it straightened out right now. If you allow a disagreement, even a minor one that happens innocently, to fester into an ongoing conflict, it is bad for your marriage and bad for your kids.

Address disagreements in private. Kids are not dumb; they can tell when you and your spouse are in conflict. But that doesn't mean they need to be spectators as you work out the problem. Take your disagreement behind closed doors, come to a solution and then announce it to the kids. And it's not "Dad's solution" or "Mom's solution"; it's "our solution." I know there were times when Jan didn't agree with a parenting decision I made, but she always waited to discuss it with me in private instead of in front of the kids. A united front helps build a sense of security in the children.

Talk about your feelings as well as the issues. Staying united during conflict is tough on both of you. In the process of sorting out the disagreement, be honest about your feelings; don't stuff them. Share them without accusing or blaming. If you feel offended, say so. If you have offended your spouse, apologize and ask forgiveness.

Confront, don't explode. Always keep your emotions under control. Angry outbursts between spouses only add more fuel to the conflict.

These next paragraphs reflect more of a wide-angle view of your relationship in general. Many disagreements and conflicts can be avoided or resolved quickly if you are continually nurturing your marriage.

Talk about your relationship. Don't be content with the status quo; keep growing as a couple. Be honest about your own needs in the relationship. It's OK to say, "I need a day away from the kids" or "We need to get away for a weekend without the kids."

Admit your weaknesses and failures to each other. Don't try to appear like you have it all together. Nobody does.

Take time to play together. Don't get so busy with parenting that you leave no time for going out on dates, occasionally getting away for weekends alone, enjoying friendships without the kids, doing projects or hobbies together and so on.

Take time for deep talk. A mom and dad's conversation at home can be dominated by their kids' needs, activities, schedules and crises. You need to go the extra mile to foster deep conversation with each other that doesn't primarily relate to parenting. Talk about your respective spiritual journeys, such as what you have been reading and praying about. Share with each other your hopes and dreams for your careers, your next home, upcoming anniversary celebrations or vacations and other opportunities on the horizon.

Be united in your parenting. Train your kids to understand that Mom and Dad are a team. Don't let them pit you against each other. Make parenting decisions in private together whenever possible. Back each other up. It may sound something like, "If your mom says no, I say no" or "Dad and I will talk about it and get back to you." Some friends of ours have problems in this area. The father feels like their little girl should be allowed to blurt out anything that's on her mind, good or bad. When she is verbally mean and disrespectful toward the mother, Dad offers no support to his wife. What do you think the child is learning from her parents' behavior?

Don't even think about divorce. With or without kids, marriage can be difficult and challenging. Stay focused on healing hurts, overcoming obstacles and growing stronger in marriage. Divorce should not be regarded as an option "just in case we can't work it out." However, with that said, I certainly realize that divorce happens in our society. The next section will offer helps for parents in that situation.

SEPARATED OR DIVORCED PARENTS

In my original outline for this book, I did not include a section addressed to divorced parents. However, after surveying so many kids from single-parent homes, I was convinced that this section was necessary. Divorce and its ramifications are a *major* issue with kids who have been touched by it. The pain of divorce that kids feel is rarely matched by any other kind of pain. If you are divorced, I hope this section is of help to you. If you are not divorced, perhaps this section will help you talk to friends who are divorced and encourage them about their parenting.

It is more important for parents who are divorced to work in harmony on their parenting than for parents who are still married. The children are already hurting from the physical and emotional breakup of the family. But you can help alleviate some of that pain by working together as parents even though you are not together.

Support your ex. It is important that you don't speak disparagingly of your ex-spouse in front of your children. It may be difficult for you to speak positively when you were deeply hurt in the divorce. It's like being fired from a job and then being asked to give a glowing testimonial for your boss at the retirement party. But for the sake of your kids, suck it up and swallow your pride and your hurt. *Never* put down your ex in your kids' hearing. *Never* use innuendo or side comments about his or her character. *Never* criticize his or her choices or decisions in front of the kids. Discuss your problems with your ex, your pastor or counselor or God, but keep the kids out of it.

Don't ask your kids to help carry your emotional baggage. You and your ex both carry emotional and possibly even physical hurt from the divorce. Don't dump any of it on the children. Don't expect them to be your confidants and support network. They have enough pain of their own to carry. Resist the temptation to plead your case to them, trying to gain their sympathy. Be aware of your own emotional fragility and find a counselor or friend to help you process it.

Find ways to make the kids feel secure. I'm not simply talking about saying things like, "I'll always take care of you." It needs to be deeper. Conveying security means a lot of physical touch so they can feel that you are there. It means checking in with them when they don't expect it so they know you're thinking about them, especially if they are living with your ex. It means standing with your ex, affirming each other in front of the kids and explaining clearly how you will manage the parenting arrangement. It means, when they are old enough, bringing the kids into the discussion about family matters and asking their opinions for handling certain issues. It means showing, by your words and actions, that nothing, not a new romantic interest or a different job or a new car or how they behave, will ever separate them from your love.

Communicate, communicate, communicate. After a divorce, many kids feel like a fifth wheel. Some of this is understandable. You want to protect them from the messy details, so you keep that part of your relationship with your ex at a distance. But you also need to find ways to talk with your kids as openly as appropriate. Don't surprise them with sudden, new information. Don't upset their lives. Keep them in the loop on decisions. They need the reassurance of your voice and your words. Share with them appropriately about what is going on in your life.

Here are a number of communication *dos* and *don'ts* for divorced parents from Brette McWhorter Sember's book *How to Parent with Your Ex*. These statements may be helpful for you and your ex to discuss together.

Things to Say to Your Child

- I love you.
- You are always going to be a part of my family.
- I am happy to be with you.
- I am so proud of the way you _____.
- I know this is difficult for you.
- I am always willing to listen to anything you need to talk about.
- This is your home as well.
- Your mother/father and I disagree about some things, and that's OK.
- Mom/Dad and I divorced each other but not you. We will always be your parents and we will work hard to parent together.
- One of the reasons we got divorced was because we disagreed about too many things. You and I can disagree and you don't have to worry that we will ever lose each other.
- Moms and Dads get divorced but parents and kids never can.
- Your Mom/Dad will always be your Mom/Dad and that's how I want it.
- This is the schedule we are going to be using. I'd like to know how you feel about it.
- Your friends are welcome to visit here at our house.
- When we are not together, I think about you and I am

happy to know I will be seeing you again soon.

- You can call Mom/Dad anytime you want to from here.
- How did your presentation go at school today?
- Where did you and your friend ride to on your bikes yesterday?
- Why don't you ask Mom/Dad to help you with that? He/She is good at things like that.
- We are not going to get back together. I know that would make you happy but the divorce is final and neither one of us wants to get back together.
- Where do you think we should go on our vacation together?
- We are using this schedule because we think it is the best way to share our time with you. We both would be with you all the time if we could, but we can't.
- It isn't anyone's fault that we got divorced. Sometimes marriages just don't work out.
- I moved out because the fighting wasn't good for any of us.
- How great that Mom/Dad took you to the zoo. What did you see there?
- I wish I could be with you all the time, too, but then you would never see Mom/Dad. It is important that we share time with you.
- This is your home too. You have two homes and it's important to me that you feel like this is a place where you live.

Communications Don'ts

- Your Mother/Father is dishonest/mean/stupid/cruel/lazy/cheap, etc.

- You are going to have to choose which parent you want to be with.
- You always side with your Mother/Father.
- You are just like your Mom/Dad.
- Ever since the divorce, I have felt so alone.
- When you leave I am all alone.
- Don't you wish you could see me more?
- Sometimes I just want to kill myself.
- I pay your Mother/Father a lot of money so you will have new clothes and he/she spends it on other things.
- If he/she doesn't think it is enough, he/she can just take me to court for more money.
- Do you know how much you are costing me each month?
- We can't go to the movies because your Mother/Father took all the money from me in the divorce.
- Who was the man/woman at the house when I picked you up?
- Tell your Mother/Father that I am not paying another dime this month.
- Where is Mom/Dad going tonight?
- Don't tell Mom/Dad we did this.
- Which one of us do you love more?
- Tell Mom/Dad that I can't pick you up until 7:00 next Friday.
- Give your Mother/Father this check and say that's all I have right now.
- Watch out for men/women. They take what they want and throw you aside.
- Don't ever get married. You'll regret it.

- I hardly ever get to see you.
- You don't even miss me. You probably don't even think about me when you're not here.
- This is the only time I get to see you and you're ignoring me?
- Why don't you call Mom/Dad and ask if you can stay a little longer.
- I'm going to win back custody of you some day.
- If you lived with me, you would be able to stay up later/buy more clothes/have parties/get a new computer/have a puppy.

I think you probably realize by now that a lack of security is often what a young person feels because of many of the Anger Generators. However, when mom and dad aren't together on issues, it probably creates more insecurity than any of the others.

CONSIDER AND RESPOND

1. What do you recall from your growing up years about your parents' harmony in raising you and your siblings? Was there some degree of conflict between them on parenting issues? How did you deal with your parents' conflict?

2. Which of the tips in this chapter for harmony between parents do you most need to put into practice? How will you implement these tips? Talk about these questions with your spouse and plan concerted action.

3. Do you see areas where conflict with your spouse has hurt your children? If so, spend some time talking to your kids about it. Apologize for hurting them. Tell them you are asking God to help you become better parents. Hug them and assure them that nothing will separate them from your love.

10   Waffling

Barbara (not her real name) came to see a counselor friend of mine with a load of problems. A Christian in her mid-thirties, Barbara was struggling in a marriage that was headed in the wrong direction. Conflicts with her husband seemed insurmountable, but she didn't believe in divorce, so she needed some answers.

During a series of counseling sessions, my friend discerned that the marriage problems were largely rooted in the load of emotional baggage Barbara brought from her upbringing. Barbara was acting out the hurt, fear and anger that had been smoldering inside her since childhood, and she was unconsciously making her husband pay for her parents' mistakes.

Barbara described her parents to the counselor using words like *locomotives* and *bombastic*. As a kid, she didn't know what to expect from them. Even though they were religious people, their actions were often the opposite of what they said they believed. Some days Mom and Dad were calm and peaceful, and some days they exploded all over her for the smallest things—or for no reason at all.

Barbara's parents' boundaries, discipline and expectations for things like completing homework and being home on time seemed to change on a whim. Sometimes she could come and go as she pleased. At other times they jumped down her throat for being late—even though she didn't know for sure what "late" meant. She could never predict how they would react to what she did or didn't do. Living constantly in fear and turmoil, Barbara learned to bury her feelings. By the time she got married, she was a powder keg of untapped emotions. Even the smallest friction with her husband touched off her pain, and it was killing their marriage.

Many of the kids I talk to are living what Barbara went through as a child. Their parents are inconsistent and unpredictable in their parenting. The boundaries and requirements of last week could change this week, without notice, and change back again next week. Kids are growing up unsure of their parents' love and acceptance because these characteristics seem to rise and fall on the basis of a parent's stress level or mood or the kid's behavior. In the process, these children, like Barbara, are ticking time bombs of anger.

ANGER GENERATOR 10:
BEING INCONSISTENT IN YOUR PARENTING

In so many areas of life, consistency is the key to success and inconsistency precipitates failure. For example, if we are inconsistent about eating the right foods and exercising regularly, we probably won't lose much weight. If we are inconsistent in the spiritual disciplines of Bible study, prayer and fellowship with other believers, it will stunt our spiritual growth and effectiveness. And for us golfers, inconsistency at maintaining the proper grip, backswing, follow-through and so on means the scores won't be as good for us.

It's the same with parenting. Being inconsistent at applying the skills of teaching, training and nurturing our kids will work against the positive results we desire for them. Inconsistency at applying the nine other anger minimizers in this book will neutralize much of their positive effect and keep the door open for hurt and anger. For example, you may resist pushing a child into a career that's not really her, but if you overly control her wardrobe or her activities, the inconsistency may stir up anger. Or if, like Barbara's parents, you allow circumstances or moods to determine how you respect, discipline, accept or favor your children, the positive things you do will be heavily discounted by your negative inconsistency.

Our inconsistency shows up in parenting primarily through the mixed messages we send to our kids. Whenever our words, actions, reactions and attitudes don't send the same message, we provoke our kids to anger. Here are some examples:

- Telling kids we love them just the way they are and then calling them "numskull" or "loser" or "dope" when they don't bring home the grades we expect

- Coming down hard on an act of misbehavior but letting the same deed slide the next time

- Saying "I love both you kids just the same" but showing more grace to the one who gives us less trouble

- Insisting that our children live within the boundaries we set for them but failing to live within healthy boundaries ourselves

- Stating boundaries for behavior but failing to consistently hold kids to them

- Threatening discipline for misbehavior but not following through or disciplining in anger

- Telling our kids about the freedom of following Christ while imposing our brand of Christianity on them

Mixed messages stir up anxiety and anger in kids because they don't know what to expect from their parents. Your kids naturally want to please you, but when you are inconsistent in your messages they will be confused about what you expect or what you want from them. These mixed messages will keep them feeling insecure and angry.

ANGER MINIMIZER 10:
STRIVING FOR CONSISTENCY IN YOUR PARENTING

Let's be clear about it from the start: There's no such thing as perfect consistency in anything where human beings are involved, including parenting. All we can hope for is to grow in consistency in our parenting. As we do, we should see a commensurate level of peace in our kids. Here are a few requirements for growing in consistency as parents.

Know your convictions. Our girls have told Jan and me that they remember us discussing the sermon on the way home from church each Sunday. According to them, this not only helped them understand our beliefs and convictions but set a pattern for them for developing their own beliefs.

Parents who have not settled or their beliefs and convictions for parenting will come across as inconsistent in their parenting. I'm talking about boundaries, discipline, showing respect, demonstrating unconditional love, allowing kids to be themselves, sharing your faith with your kids and other values. Many parents tend to make decisions on the fly or from emotions instead of working from a plan. In order to work from a plan, you must have identified your convictions ahead of time.

Communicate regularly with your spouse. Parenting from convictions should be a team effort. This is true even if you are divorced; it's just more difficult when you're not under the same roof. You need to understand each other's convictions so you can present a united front. Periodically talk through the anger generators and anger minimizers in this book with your spouse or ex. Talk about your personal beliefs and convictions in these areas. Admit where you have been inconsistent and discuss how you can be more consistent in each area. Regular communication on these issues will reveal where you disagree in your parenting. Use these discoveries to find ways to amicably compromise for the good of the children. Keep working with each other so that your messages to the kids—words, actions, follow-through, examples, etc.— sound and feel the same.

Keep your emotions in check. Most of our discussion on consistency has focused on our actions—what we do in response to the parenting challenges our kids present to us. But every challenge sparks some kind of emotion in us: anger, anxiety, impatience, fear, etc. If you fail to keep your emotions under control, you may catch your kids off guard because they don't know what to expect from you emotionally. Inconsistent emotions from a parent can be just as harmful to kids as inconsistent actions.

I tended to "let it all hang out" emotionally with our kids. When I was ticked off at them and their behavior, it usually showed. One of our daughters thought that Jan was a bit "too controlled" in these settings. She knew there were times when Mom should be a little angry and wanted to see her "get fired up a little."

So much of what your children learn from you comes through your display of emotions. How you respond emotionally may not minimize the importance of what you say, but your emotions could conflict with your words or action, resulting in inconsistency. Emotions are neither right nor wrong in themselves, but if we lose control of how we express them, it can be harmful to our children

Be honest about your inconsistency. We all realize that achieving consistency in parenting is a matter of gradual improvement interspersed with numerous failures. We must admit our lapses in consistency, apologize to our spouses and/or children when we are guilty of them and forgive family members when they are inconsistent. When you admit your weakness and mistakes to your kids, it will help clear up mixed messages and help them feel more secure.

At one point in the development of my hobby of golf I became so frustrated with my inconsistent play that I decided to take lessons from a golf pro. During the first lesson, my teacher asked why I had signed up.

"I've been diligent about going to the driving range to practice my swing," I began. "But it dawned on me that I was simply practicing the bad habits I was already using. Being on the driving range was hurting my game more than helping it. I think I need to learn some *good* habits to practice."

My teacher agreed. And the lessons have helped me build some consistency in the right direction.

Like me on the driving range, perhaps you are struggling with success in your parenting because you have been practicing the wrong skills. Your kids may not be responding the way you hoped. They may be sullen, distant or even angry. It may be that you have been consistent while using the wrong tactics.

I hope you have found in this book a number of good skills you can start working on in your home. Being consistent is vital to your success in parenting, but only if you're consistent in doing the right things.

CONSIDER AND RESPOND

1. In what areas were your parents generally consistent in parenting you and your siblings? In what areas were they inconsistent? How do you think your parents' consistency and inconsistency affected your development?

2. In what areas do you have the most difficulty being consistent as a parent? What tip from this chapter has been most helpful to you for developing greater consistency?

3. Sit down with your spouse or ex-spouse soon and discuss the areas where you need to be more consistent with your children. If you discover differences in convictions or values, seek to find a compromise you can both commit to.

Just Keep Them Dancing

When Riverdance performed in Denver for the first time several years ago, the Irish dance troupe was on the front edge of the explosive popularity it still enjoys around the world. The promoters of the Denver show decided that our NBA basketball facility, McNichols Arena, was the perfect venue. The arena seats 15,000 for basketball, and another 2,000-3,000 chairs were set up on the floor for the dance performances. Since the floor seats were closest to the stage, they were the most expensive.

There was just one little problem. The surface of the stage was five feet off the floor, so most of the people who paid big bucks for floor seats could only see the dancers from the waist up! Now, if you've never seen Riverdance, you need to know that most of what people go to see is happening on the floor. This awe-inspiring art is called step dancing. It's all about agile, precision footwork while the dancers' hands and arms are relatively motionless. If you can only see the performers from the belt up, you've missed most of the show. Needless to say, in Denver there were more than a few refunds demanded from those in the expensive floor seats.

When it comes to parenting your children, you may feel at times like you are watching the action from those seats on the floor. For all the time, energy and resources you put into it, you can see what's happening on the surface but not much of what's being accomplished on the inside as a result of your investment. And it's easy to get down on yourself based on your limited perspective, wondering if you're doing something wrong and if your kids are going to turn out all right.

Let me offer some encouragement from the "cheap seats." During nearly four decades in youth ministry I've heard the same concerns from parents just like you. But I've also heard the rest of the story in countless numbers of cases. The years went by, the parents hung in there, the kids grew up, and the overwhelming majority of them turned out just fine—and their parents did too. You may be too close to the action to see it right now, but your kids are going to be OK too.

What is the common denominator for success? In my experience, I could phrase it this way: Just keep them dancing. In other words, just keep doing the right things in the right way, especially the anger minimizers in this book. You can't see everything that's happening inside them—how they're developing, changing, growing and getting it together. But I can tell you that you will see the best part eventually. Your efforts will pay off. This doesn't mean there won't be problems, but over time you will have the opportunity to see your kids blossom.

So hang in there, and may you have God's wisdom in the process.

NOTES

CHAPTER 3: PLAYING FAVORITES

p. 42   Blocked quote: Kevin Leman, *The New Birth Order Book: Why You Are the Way You Are,* 2nd ed.(Grand Rapids: Revell, 1998), p. 15.

CHAPTER 4: HEY DUMMY!

p. 49   Quote from Neil Clark Warren: *Make Anger Your Ally* (Brentwood, Tenn.: Wolgemuth & Hyatt, 1990), p. 121.

pp. 50-51   Blocked quote: Gary Smalley and Greg Smalley, *The DNA of Parent-Teen Relationships* (Wheaton, Ill.: Tyndale House Publishers, 2005), pp. 35-36.

p. 53   "Deciding to place": Ibid., p. 17.

p. 53   Blocked quote with bullet points: Ibid., pp. 21-30.

p. 54   Chart: Foster Cline and Jim Fay, *Parenting with Love & Logic: Teaching Children Responsibility* (Colorado Springs: Piñon Press, 2006), p. 61.

CHAPTER 5: A WORLD WITHOUT BOUNDARIES

p. 62   Seven cries list: Timothy Smith, *The Seven Cries of Today's Teens* (Nashville: Integrity Publishers, 2003), p. 22.

pp. 67-68   Boundary guidelines: Summarized from Henry Cloud and John Townsend, *Boundaries with Kids* (Grand Rapids: Zondervan, 2001), pp. 42-43.

CHAPTER 6: CRIME AND PUNISHMENT

p. 76   "The more we give": Foster Cline and Jim Fay, *Parenting with Love & Logic: Teaching Children Responsibility* (Colorado Springs: Piñon Press, 2006), p. 72.

p. 77   "Children who grow": Sylvia B. Rimm, *How to Parent So Children Will Learn* (Watertown, Wis.: Apple Publishing, 1990), quoted in Foster Cline and Jim Fay, *Parenting with Love & Logic: Teaching Children Responsibility* (Colorado Springs: Piñon Press, 2006), p. 74.

p. 77   "The sides of the 'V'": Cline and Fay, *Parenting with Love*, p. 75.

p. 77   Blocked quote with bullet points: Ibid., p. 78.

pp. 77-81   Case study: Adapted from ibid., pp. 78-83.

CHAPTER 9: THE TWO-HEADED MONSTER

pp. 111-14   Blocked list with bullet points: Brette McWorter Sember, *How to Parent with Your Ex* (Naperville, Ill.: Sphinx Publications, 2005), pp. 25-28.